COLORFUL
CHARACTERS
OF
PITTSBURGH

COLORFUL
CHARACTERS
OF
PITTSBURGH

PAUL KING

THE
History
PRESS

Published by The History Press
Charleston, SC
www.historypress.com

First published 2023

Manufactured in the United States

ISBN 9781467148580

Library of Congress Control Number: 2023938362

*This book is dedicated to Chris, Jeff, Pete and Kevin,
four great sons and each colorful in his own way.*

CONTENTS

ACKNOWLEDGEMENTS

As always, I am indebted to my friends for their assistance in completing this book: Bob and Maggie Holder, for giving the chapters a read and suggesting edits; David E. Martin, for his moral support and advice; to everyone who helped me compile the list and whittle it down through their suggestions; and to my acquisitions editor, J. Banks Smither, for sticking by me through what turned out to be a more arduous process than I had ever imagined. Finally, to my wife, Karen, who is always there for me in "good times and bum times," in the immortal words of Stephen Sondheim.

INTRODUCTION

When I began to do the research for *Colorful Characters of Pittsburgh*, I had only a fair sense of who I wanted to include. My template was basically the suggestions I had received from people while planning *Iconic Pittsburgh: The City's 30 Most Memorable People, Places and Things*. They were names that some Pittsburghers considered local icons, and some undoubtedly would have been included had I been able to write a longer book.

They were people such as Porky Chedwick, the "Daddio of the Raddio" beginning in the 1950s, the disc jockey who set the standard for both radio and "sock hops" and then kept raising the bar; Myron Cope, the nasal-voiced sportscaster who created an icon of his own when he came up with the idea for the "Terrible Towel" in 1975; Vic Cianca, the traffic cop who gained national recognition because of his ballet-like way of directing cars and trucks through the Golden Triangle's busiest intersections; and Robert Lansberry, the homeless protester who paraded up and down the streets of downtown Pittsburgh with sandwich boards decrying government "mind control" and the Federal Bureau of Investigation's purloining of his mail.

As I studied these names, I saw a thread that seemed to tie them together. Each of them was cut from an unconventional cloth. They were bold, brash, outspoken and one of a kind. They were the sort of people some would call "colorful." And that became my hook.

Using those men as my base, I dug into newspaper archives and local history books to build on it. And, of course, I turned to my friends and relatives on Facebook to ask them to throw out the names of other people they thought might be "colorful" enough for inclusion.

The list I settled on comprises a diverse cast of characters. They range from the homeless to the well-off, from saints to sinners, from athletes to broadcasters to fans and from stars of radio, TV and the internet to those whose stories unfolded before any of those media had been conceived.

There are a select few whose fame, or infamy, spread across the country—and sometimes the globe. Nellie Bly (born Elizabeth Jane Cochran in 1864), the crusading journalist and world traveler from nearby Apollo, got her start at the *Pittsburgh Dispatch* newspaper, and Kate Soffel, the love-struck warden's wife, gained national notoriety by helping two brothers escape from her husband's jail. There is Dr. Cyril H. Wecht, the medical examiner whose expertise has been sought by lawyers and law enforcement agencies throughout the fifty states, and Dante "Tex" Gill, the transgender massage parlor operator and mob figure who, in the 1970s, was also sought by law enforcement, but for an entirely different reason.

Figures such as Sophie Masloff, Rege Cordic, Ed and Wendy King and Edgar Snyder forged a path in one way or another by attempting, or achieving, something no one had managed before them. Others—like Curt Wootton, Rick Sebak, Gus Kalaris and Randy Gilson—manifest their love for the city in the work they do, while transplants such as Mike Lange, Bob Prince and Dock Ellis grew to love and appreciate the people of Pittsburgh.

Each of the people profiled in this book has been intricately woven into the expansive quilt that makes up the history of this awesome city. As much as Andrew Carnegie, H.J. Heinz, Art Rooney, Fred Rogers, Mary Schenley and August Wilson, they all have left their mark on Pittsburgh.

Part I

THE POLITICAL AND THE CRIMINAL

Joe Barker: The "Accidental" Mayor

You might think that being a convicted criminal would put a serious crimp in a person's political aspirations, and most times you would be right. But in 1849, the arrest and conviction of a Pittsburgh "street preacher" actually was the catalyst that propelled the man into the mayor's seat.

Joe Barker, who served for one tumultuous year as the city's top government official, did dabble in politics prior to his election as mayor. The resident of Bayardstown was elected sheriff for a time in the early 1840s. But what Barker really liked to do was rage against the ills of the country, or at least what he thought were the nation's problems. Barker, a married man with two children, was a self-appointed preacher possessed of a fiery temper and spewing equally incendiary oratory, and there were few subjects he wouldn't tackle in his "sermons."

Barker identified as a nativist, a quasi-political group that favored descendants of the original thirteen colonies over later immigrants. Not only was he anti-immigrant, but he also was virulently anti-Catholic. Much of his vitriol was directed at Irish and Italian settlers. Barker opposed the Freemasons as well and railed against slavery, the abuse of alcohol and political and police corruption. Those latter causes, of course, did not exactly endear him to the members of city hall.

Barker was easily recognizable in his signature black cape and stovepipe hat, as well as by the fact that he was clean-shaven—a rarity for the time.

Joseph Barker.
Wikimedia Commons.

He could be found at least twice a week choosing one or another prominent street corner in downtown Pittsburgh to address his broad political agenda. But whatever the subject, listeners to a Barker speech were guaranteed to be subjected to vulgar and offensive language, as well as to his rowdy entourage. Nonetheless, Barker managed to draw good-sized crowds whenever he spoke.

When John Herron was elected mayor in January 1849, Barker quickly became the proverbial thorn in Herron's side, just as he had been to William J. Howard, Dr. William Kerr and Gabriel Adams, the mayors who immediately preceded Herron. (Mayoral elections, which were first held in 1836, were staged annually until 1868.)

But of course, Barker's speeches were protected by the First Amendment of the U.S. Constitution, so even if his language was considered vulgar and his messages sometimes abhorrent, there was little the politicians or police could do about the content of Barker's speeches.

But as Barker's supporters grew in number and in boldness, businesspeople also became more vocal in their complaints about the preacher. Sometimes the crowds were so large and rowdy that shoppers had difficulty getting into stores. Finally, after a particularly boisterous event on Friday, September 14, 1849, Herron got his chance. He had Barker arrested, along with two cohorts, Hugh Kirkland and John Sharp. The charges were disturbing the peace by using lewd and indecent language, blocking traffic and inciting a riot.

In early November, the three men went on trial, during which Barker certainly did little to help his case. He threatened the jury and promised to hang Judge Benjamin Patton "from a lamppost" if he got the chance. The three men were convicted on all counts, and on November 19, Barker was sentenced to twelve months in jail and fined $250. (On that day, sentencing for Kirkland and Sharp was postponed. A search of newspaper accounts did not reveal what punishment those two men received, suggesting that reporters either lost interest or were too busy focusing their reportage on Barker to care about the other defendants.)

But if Herron thought he had solved his problem, he soon discovered how wrong he was. Even before the sentencing, Barker's supporters had launched a grassroots campaign to have their man added to the 1850 mayoral ballot. They weren't successful, but that didn't stop them. They simply took their campaign to the streets, exhorting everyone to write in Barker's name on the ballot. Amazingly, it worked. When the smoke cleared on January 2, 1850, Barker had garnered 1,787 votes, 203 more than the Democratic candidate, John B. Guthrie.

To say that officials were red-faced with embarrassment is grossly understating the situation. Their city's newly elected mayor was languishing in jail, and they were forced to ask Governor William Johnston for a pardon, which he granted. But when the governor's telegram announcing his decision arrived, the city council decided that it would be prudent to wait for the official document to be delivered before releasing Barker. That decision proved problematic when Inauguration Day arrived and the document hadn't. Barker's supporters were livid, and a mob threatened to attack the jail and break Barker out. In the end, the city agreed to release Barker long enough to be sworn in. (In a final ironic twist, the man chosen to conduct the swearing-in was Judge Patton, who had sentenced Barker to jail in the first place. Some reports suggest that Barker actually requested Patton for the ceremony.) After he was sworn in, the new mayor was escorted back to his cell. The next day, the pardon was received, and Barker was a free man.

As mayor, Barker continued to be a man at war against the system, as he tried to bend it to his will. Unlike former mayors, Barker refused to turn a blind eye to corruption. He went after vendors who "weighted" scales in order to cheat customers. He enforced a ten-hour workday. He cracked down on various forms of gambling and had no tolerance for public drunkenness.

"Although his politics were questionable, he did have some good qualities," said Robert Barker, Joe's great-great-great-grandson, who is a professor emeritus of law at Duquesne University. "As mayor he cleaned up the 'red light' district and he cleaned up the marketplace." However, Barker—who is Catholic—explained that it is tough to admire his Methodist ancestor because of his anti-Catholic harangues.

Unfortunately, Barker's good intentions were undone by his methods. His answer to police corruption was to try to fire all the city's policemen and replace them with his own hires. However, without the backing of the city council, the situation devolved into a tale of two police forces, with Barker's men and the established police force fighting continually. His efforts to settle a custody dispute ended with him being arrested and charged with child abduction. He assaulted alleged criminals on several occasions, threatening to kill one suspect. As a result, he found himself in court twice to answer assault and battery charges.

When the results of the 1851 election were announced, Barker found himself a distant third. His mayoralty was over, and he would never again hold public office. He ran twice more for mayor and a few times for sheriff. But the rest of his days were spent back on the streets, in his preacher's garb, doing just what he had done before he rose to power. When he wasn't attacking Catholics or speaking out against slavery, he was leading the opposition in trying to prevent the merger of Pittsburgh and Allegheny City. (In this, at least, he had much support. Allegheny was not annexed by Pittsburgh until 1907.) When he wasn't preaching, more often than not he was in jail; his passion and hatred never abated in all his adult life.

Joe Barker's story came to an unexpected, and grisly, end on August 2, 1862, at the age of fifty-five. Heading home that evening, reportedly after attending a rally supporting the Union cause during the Civil War, Barker was walking along railroad tracks in the Manchester section when a train struck and decapitated him.

Of course, politicians are seldom forgotten, especially one as controversial and outspoken as Joe Barker. Aside from the expected mentions of him in articles about the history of the Pittsburgh mayoralty, Barker's past came up a few times in news reports years after his death.

In 2007, the *Pittsburgh Catholic* newspaper invoked the ex-mayor in a column written by the paper's general manager, Robert P. Lockwood. In the article, Lockwood castigated Spencer Gifts, the owners of the Spirit Halloween Store in Pleasant Hills, for selling as costumes nuns' habits with sexual themes. He likened the costumes' sale to the anti-Catholicism that was promoted by a portion of society in mid-nineteenth-century Pittsburgh.

Lockwood's prime example of that religious hatred were the attacks of Joe Barker against Bishop Michael O'Connor in 1846, when the latter announced the opening of the city's first hospital. Barker and his followers were aghast that the hospital was to be run by the Sisters of Mercy, an order of Irish nuns. As mayor, Barker even had O'Connor arrested over what the mayor said was a sewage issue with the hospital.

Lockwood wrote, "Perhaps on occasion we'll offer a little award in [Barker's] name to those who persist in the kind of mindless anti-Catholicism so reflective of his short term as mayor. For peddling offensive Halloween costumes of nuns, let's give the first Joe Barker Memorial Award to Spencer Gifts. They can hang it by the lava lamps."

Lockwood also provided an ironic postscript to Barker's life. A few years later, at a "Celebration of Catholic Pittsburgh," Lockwood spoke about the column. He explained that a few days after the column ran, he received a letter from Robert Barker, explaining his relationship to the former mayor and noting with irony that he, Robert, was an active member of the Catholic Church.

"I think of old Joe Barker and what he would think of a great-great-great-grandson who had been raised to be a staunch and devout Catholic," Lockwood noted.

There was one other reference to the ex-mayor discovered in news accounts, and it was an unfortunate one for a man named Harry Barker. In March 1948, Harry Barker died at the age of seventy-eight. The death of the house painter, of natural causes in a rooming house on the Northside, probably would have gone unremarked on if it hadn't been for the fact that he was reportedly identified by his daughter as the son of Joe Barker. The *Pittsburgh Press* noted his passing the day after his death with a short piece headlined "Son of Ex-Mayor Dies on North Side," and then revisited the story the following day, giving over about eight column-inches of space in a piece headlined "Like Fiery Mayor-Father, Barker Dies in Obscurity."

Most of this article was devoted not to Harry but to Joe Barker and his history. Dredging up the past was bad enough, but a quick calculation by the editors would have revealed that Harry was born eight years after Joe Barker died. So, while Harry may have been the ex-mayor's grandson, he could not have been his son.

Robert Barker noted that although his knowledge of the family tree is incomplete, he does not recall any mention of a Harry Barker in family archives or conversation.

Interestingly, the reporter wrote that "neighbors didn't know the story of the stormy career of his father" and added that the son "did nothing to revive [the story]." For obvious reasons, as it turns out.

NELLIE BLY: AROUND THE WORLD AS A JOURNALIST

Parents looking for a role model for their daughters would do well to teach them about Nellie Bly. Whether it was traveling around the world alone to prove a point or getting herself confined to an insane asylum in the cause of investigative journalism, Nellie Bly was definitely a strong-willed woman ahead of her time. From a young age, she knew that she did not want to be the typical wife, mother and homemaker, and as soon as she was able, she set out to pursue some unconventional dreams.

In her lifetime, she would become a top-flight muckraking reporter, prove herself to be a savvy world traveler and even manage to invent a few items while managing a manufacturing company.

"People really know her as being a champion for mental health," said Beth Caldwell, executive director of Pittsburgh Professional Women. "But she was a champion for everything: Mexican Americans, immigrants, women. What I love about Nellie and other women of her time was how brave they were and how scary it must have been. But thank God they did that. They paved the way for the rest of us."

But there was little in Bly's childhood to suggest that she would be capable of such feats. Bly was born Elizabeth Jane Cochran in the small town of Cochran's Mills, about fifty miles northeast of Pittsburgh. Her father, Michael Cochran, was the owner of the mill for which the town was named and also an Armstrong County judge. So, the Cochrans should have lived a comfortable life.

But Michael died unexpectedly in 1870, when Elizabeth was only six. Worse, he had not prepared a will. With fifteen children—ten from his first wife and five with Mary Jane Kennedy, his second spouse and Elizabeth's mother—his estate was divided among all his progeny. Mary Jane suddenly had very little with which to raise her children. They moved to Apollo, and Mary Jane remarried. But she soon left her abusive spouse, and the family struggled.

Nellie Bly. *Wikimedia Commons.*

Elizabeth planned to become a teacher to support herself and her mother. At fifteen, she enrolled at Indiana Normal School (now Indiana University of Pennsylvania), but she was forced to leave after a year because she couldn't afford the tuition. She and her mother relocated to Pittsburgh, where two of Elizabeth's brothers lived.

But the young Miss Cochrane, who added the *e* to the end of her surname in order to sound more sophisticated, found it difficult to land a job. Women in the workplace were most often found doing the most menial jobs, and Elizabeth aspired to much loftier heights. Elizabeth's career path finally began to take shape in 1885, and it was unwittingly created by one of the city's most outspoken chauvinists. That year, Erasmus Wilson, considered by some to be the city's preeminent newspaper writer, wrote a column in the *Pittsburgh Dispatch* titled "What Girls Are Good For." In it, he called working women "a monstrosity" and suggested that their time would be better spent by making "home a little paradise" and being "an angel" to their husbands.

Elizabeth was incensed at the column. She fired off a letter to the editor advocating for more employment opportunities for women. She signed the letter "Lonely Orphan Girl." Managing editor George Madden was impressed with the moxie the twenty-year-old demonstrated. He placed an ad in the newspaper asking for "Orphan Girl" to contact him and identify herself.

Elizabeth did—by showing up in Madden's office the next day. He asked her to craft an article that showed "the women's sphere," based on the letter she had written. The *Dispatch* published the article, for which Elizabeth was paid. After Elizabeth wrote a second opinion piece, on divorce, Madden offered her a job. Her salary, five dollars per week, would be a pittance compared to what male reporters received. On top of that, she would have to come up with a pseudonym—it wasn't "proper" for female writers to reveal their own names.

Elizabeth took the job and even agreed to accept the name the other reporters came up with: Nellie Bly. The men must have thought they were being clever, as the name comes from an 1850 Stephen Foster song about a Black servant named Nelly Bly who was content to do all the household chores she was assigned. But Elizabeth Cochrane would prove that she was the antithesis of Nelly Bly; in fact, she would fight her whole life to raise the status of women.

Working at the *Dispatch*, Nellie told the stories of the lives of factory workers, reporting on their low wages, long hours and unsafe working conditions. Her articles garnered a ton of attention, as well as a lot of ire from local companies, some of them advertisers. They made their displeasure known, and the editors decided that it would be best if Miss Bly were given a more "traditional" job. So, Madden transferred her to the women's and society pages.

As you might imagine, Nellie was not happy about this, and she looked for any way out. She begged for the chance to travel to Mexico, where she could report on international issues for the *Dispatch*. She spent six months traveling throughout Mexico, reporting on women's issues, the plight of the poor and the corruption within the Mexican government.

The results were predictable. Incensed Mexican officials had her thrown out of the country. A male reporter might have been allowed to wear that expulsion like a badge of honor. Nellie was punished with consignment back to the society pages.

By this time, Nellie had figured that Pittsburgh was just too small and parochial to allow newspapers to work past gender issues and use her talents fully. So, in 1887, she decided to seek her future in New York City. Brimming with the confidence of someone who has little to lose and fueled by the frustration of a person who has had doors slammed in her face for her whole life, Nellie headed to the *New York World* and barged into the office of its editor, Joseph Pulitzer. She was prepared with a story pitch, a series on the immigrant experience in the United States. Pulitzer fired back with a proposal of his own: an investigation into New York's mental "health" system—specifically, conditions on Blackwell's Island, the city's most notorious insane asylum.

If his intention was to scare off this twenty-three-year-old would-be journalist, his plan backfired in awesome fashion. Nellie accepted the challenge. What's more, she accomplished the job by faking a mental illness and getting herself committed to Blackwell's Island. She not only witnessed the horrors of this asylum, she experienced them herself as well. Ten days later, lawyers from the *World* secured her release, and Nellie had the story that would make her famous.

"Ten Days in the Madhouse" ran as a six-part series in the *World* and later was turned into a book. It arguably was also the beginning of what we know today as investigative journalism. Over the next two years, Nellie would tackle such subjects as corruption in government and even the practice of selling babies on the black market. Her place in history was cemented by the age of twenty-five.

But Nellie Bly was always looking for the next challenge, the next opportunity to prove that women could be as driven, as courageous and as resourceful as men. So, in 1888, Nellie suggested to managing editor John Cockerill that she attempt to travel around the world—alone—in order to prove not only that it could be done but also that it could be done by a woman in less time than Jules Verne fantasized about in his 1872 novel *Around the World in Eighty Days*.

Cockerill and his team put off the headstrong Bly for as long as they could. They loved the idea, but virtually everyone at the *World* thought that a man should go; for one thing, they said, a man would need much less baggage than a woman, which only raised Nellie's hackles even more. Finally, she broke the logjam by telling Cockerill to go ahead and send a man. "I'll start the same day for some other newspaper, and beat him." Cockerill gave in.

On November 14, 1889, Bly set sail for England from New York. But it wasn't long before her journey would turn into a race. *Cosmopolitan*, then a newly minted magazine, decided to send its own traveler to try to beat Bly. As if to keep the playing field level, *Cosmopolitan*'s owner, John Brisben Walker, chose twenty-eight-year-old Elizabeth Bisland, one of the magazine's editors. Walker sent Bisland in the opposite direction as Bly, believing that traveling west was the faster way to go.

As it would turn out, both women would best the time of the fictional Phileas Fogg. But Bly would arrive back in New York on January 25, 1890, seventy-two days after she left and four days ahead of Bisland. Bly told her story in the book *Around the World in 72 Days*.

Of course, records are made to be broken, and it was only months later that the aptly named George Francis Train circumnavigated the globe in sixty-seven days. But that didn't matter to Nellie. She just went on with her life. She left the *World* and began writing serial novels for the *New York Family Story Paper*.

In 1895, Nellie married Robert Seaman, who owned Iron Clad Manufacturing Company. There was a forty-two-year difference in their ages, and Bly left her career behind to help her husband run the business, as Elizabeth Cochrane Seaman. She assumed control of the company in 1904, when her husband died, and became an inventor, coming up with a new type of milk can and a stacking garbage can. But she lacked real knowledge

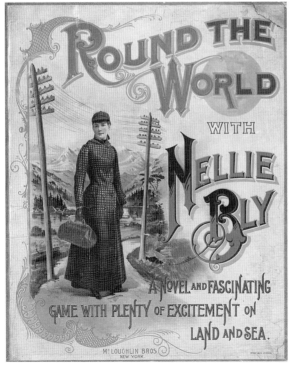

Above: Nellie Bly's headstone, Woodlawn Cemetery, Bronx, New York. *Wikimedia Commons.*

Left: Cover of a board game created by McLoughlin Bros. based on Nellie Bly's travels. *Wikimedia Commons.*

of business finances, a problem exacerbated by the embezzlement of several hundred thousand dollars by a factory manager. Iron Clad went bankrupt, and Nellie went back to work as a reporter.

She continued to report on social issues and interviewed several important figures. She became the first female reporter to report from the front lines of World War I. In 1913, when she covered the Women's Suffrage Parade in Washington, D.C., she accurately predicted that women would be given the right to vote in 1920.

For all her notoriety, when Nellie Bly died in 1922, she was buried in a pauper's grave in the Honeysuckle section of Woodlawn Cemetery in the Bronx. (Interestingly, Woodlawn is also the burial site of her former boss, Joseph Pulitzer, and her one-time rival, Elizabeth Bisland.)

Her grave didn't receive a headstone until 1978, when the New York Press Club purchased one for her. It reads:

Dedicated June 22, 1978
To
Nellie Bly
Elizabeth Cochrane Seaman
By the New York Press Club
In Honor Of
A Famous News Reporter

FATHER JAMES COX: THE ORIGINAL LABOR PRIEST

Most Pittsburghers born in the 1940s, '50s or '60s probably remember or know of Monsignor Charles Owen Rice. Father Rice, a Catholic priest, served for nearly seventy years in the Diocese of Pittsburgh. He was most well known for his pro-worker and anti-war activism. He was known as the "Labor Priest."

But Father Rice merely carried the mantle of his mentor, the original "Labor Priest," Father James Cox. A native of the city, Cox was ordained from St. Vincent Seminary in 1911 and served in various roles both here and abroad for forty years, until his untimely death in 1951.

Cox truly was a priest for the people. He fought for the rights of workers and sought help for the homeless and the hungry, so much so that in 1932 he vied for the U.S. presidency in order to effect change on a national level.

James Cox was destined to be a voice for the poor and the working class because he knew both poverty and hard work all his life. Even while he was going to school, he worked to help bring money into the household. Paper boy, store clerk, even a supervisor for a taxicab company were jobs the young Cox performed.

Early on in his ministry, the diocesan hierarchy knew that it had someone special in Father Cox. After his ordination, he was assigned as an assistant at Epiphany Church at the base of the Hill District. When the United States entered World War I, Cox enlisted and served as a chaplain at Base Hospital No. 27 in Mongoson, France. When he returned from the war, the diocese assigned him to be chaplain of Mercy Hospital. He served there until 1923, when Archbishop John Francis Canevin appointed him pastor of Old St. Patrick's Parish in the Strip District. At the age of thirty-seven, Cox was the youngest priest ever given charge of a parish. Cox used to joke that he was the youngest pastor at the city's oldest parish—St. Patrick's was founded in 1808.

Cox himself certainly believed that God had ordained him for some special purpose. While he was studying at St. Vincent's, he began to suffer from deteriorating eyesight. Doctors told him that he would eventually go blind. Cox prayed to Our Lady of Lourdes, promising that if his sight were restored, he would lead devotions to Our Lady and lead pilgrimages to Lourdes. Water from Lourdes was procured and poured on his eyes, and Cox did regain full use of his eyes.

Through fate or divine providence, the location of St. Patrick's would establish Cox's life's work: ministering to the poor and homeless and fighting for the rights of workers. In the 1920s, the Strip District was filled with empty warehouses but few businesses. Parishioners were the working poor, who were about to be dealt a devastating blow with the stock market crash of 1929.

A section of the Strip became known as "Shantytown," where hundreds of homeless and jobless people gathered in makeshift housing. Cox became known as their "mayor," as he worked tirelessly to feed as many of them as possible. With the help of local businesses and the media, he established the Father Cox Relief Fund to raise money to fund his soup kitchens.

But Cox knew that soup kitchens were the equivalent of the proverb "Give a man a fish…." So, Cox fought long and hard in talks with business people and politicians, trying to convince them to create more jobs. But the talks went nowhere, and Cox knew that a more visible approach was needed.

So, in late 1931, St. Patrick's pastor began to organize the poor and destitute in order to make a statement. He felt he needed to show business

Father James Renshaw Cox. *Cox Papers, University of Pittsburgh.*

people—and the government, starting with President Herbert Hoover—exactly who these jobless people were. In a rally held at Pitt Stadium, Cox urged men to rally together for a march on Washington, D.C. He set January 5, 1932, as the date to begin the march.

Cox arranged transportation for about 2,500 people. He was shocked—and, no doubt, overjoyed—when five times that many men showed up. The Jubilee Army, as it became known, set off for D.C., with men taking turns walking and riding as they made their way through heavy rainfall to Huntington, Pennsylvania. From there they traveled to Harrisburg and then down through Maryland to reach the nation's capital. Along the way, they received help from some unexpected sources.

For example, financier Andrew Mellon, then Hoover's secretary of the treasury, arranged for service stations to supply the marchers with gasoline for their vehicles. (The gesture would lead to an angry Hoover removing Mellon from his post.) In Harrisburg, Governor Gifford Pinchot opened the restaurant in the capitol building for the marchers and covered the expense out of his own pocket. In Washington, arrangements were made for the men, whose number had doubled by then, to be fed from army field kitchens.

Cox got the opportunity to address Congress and meet with President Hoover. Cox presented the House and Senate with a Resolution of the Jobless, in which he asked for $5 billion for public works projects, with additional money to be set aside for the unemployed and for farmers. To President Hoover, Cox compared the federal government to "an ostrich that sticks its head in the sand" in a futile attempt to hide from the problem.

Congress seemed sympathetic, but Cox made little headway with the president. In late spring, Cox decided to form his own political party, the Jobless Party, and run for president under a platform of creating public works projects, unemployment insurance, pensions for retired workers, a thirty-hour workweek and workers' right to form unions.

Of course, there never having been a Catholic as president, let alone a Catholic priest in the office, Cox was hit with many questions about his religion. Personally, he felt that it wasn't important. In fact, many of his relatives weren't even Catholic; they were Methodist. (His father was Methodist, and his mother was Catholic.) As he once explained to a reporter, "I have an old aunt who lives in our convent, and she attends Calvary Methodist Church every Sunday. I have no more ardent supporters than my Protestant relatives."

Unfortunately, as it is with most third-party candidates, Cox was ultimately undone by a lack of money and the rigors of running a meaningful national campaign with a small staff. In October, he abandoned the race and threw his support to Franklin Delano Roosevelt.

But Cox's Army had made its case. Roosevelt trounced Hoover in the November election, and the new president put into action much of what the Labor Priest had asked for. The Jobless Party broke up, leaving Cox not only as its only presidential candidate but also as the only Catholic priest in U.S. history to run for president.

Cox continued to fight for, and tend to, the poor, the jobless and the destitute. He also honored his pledge to Our Lady of Lourdes by leading regular pilgrimages to France. He also installed a grotto in the St. Patrick courtyard that was inspired by the grotto at Lourdes. Mass was broadcast on WJAS radio from St. Patrick's every Sunday, keeping Father Cox in the spotlight. The broadcasts continued even after his death, up until 1958. In the 1930s, he was a member of the Pennsylvania Commission for the Unemployed, and President Roosevelt also appointed him to the state board of the National Recovery Administration.

Father Cox was often in the newspapers, but he was definitely not a fan of them. In 1940, he suggested on one of his Sunday radio programs that newspapers should be answerable to the government, such as the way the Federal Communication Commission oversees radio. Stating that he believed newspapers were exceeding the limits of the First Amendment, he called for newspapers that "like radio, will be fair to a Roosevelt and a Wilkie, a rich man or a poor man, that will be fair and free and serve the people."

Father Cox died in 1951 after suffering a stroke, but not before he was able to meet and guide a young Charles Rice into following his footsteps. Cox's life has been preserved in the James R. Cox Collection, maintained by the Archives Service Center at the University of Pittsburgh. The collection has tapes of his radio broadcast, his diaries and manuscripts and hundreds of photographs and newspaper and magazine clippings.

Dante "Tex" Gill: Transgender Criminal

One has to wonder how Lois Jean Gill would have fared as an adult had she been born at the turn of the New Millennium rather than in 1930. Certainly her transition from a woman to a man would have gone a bit more smoothly. Probably Dante "Tex" Gill would have been more easily accepted as a man by some segments of society.

As it was, police, politicians and the media didn't know what to make of the short, frumpy person who wore men's clothing, spoke in a deep, fairly raspy voice and insisted on being called a man. Some newspapers did just that, referring to Gill as "the woman who prefers to be known as a man." Other, less accommodating media just went with biological sex and called Gill "she." Even Gill's one-time lawyer, Carl Max Janavitz, referred to Gill as "she" when he was interviewed for Gill's obituary.

However people referred to him, Tex Gill was one of the more colorful characters to frequent the local news in the 1970s and '80s. Born Lois Jean Gill in 1930 to Walter and Agnes Gill of Brookline, he likely felt more like a man from an early age. Short, stout and strong, Gill got a job in the 1950s at the stables in Schenley Park, shoeing horses and giving riding lessons. As he got older, he got into other businesses, including a furniture store and a frozen foods company, but somehow he eventually became involved in prostitution.

The sex business, and organized crime in general, became a full-time endeavor for Gill in 1964, when Agnes Gill developed cancer and young Gill needed more money to care for his mother. Gill was a minor player in Pittsburgh's crime scene for nearly a decade and a half. Eventually, he became the manager of the Spartacus massage parlor—a brothel in disguise. Under the guidance of reputed Pittsburgh crime boss George Lee, Gill learned the ins and outs of operating the sex business. The FBI arrested him once, in 1974, but couldn't make charges stick. Gill's life as a bit player might have continued indefinitely had it not been for the daylight assassination of George Lee in 1977. Gill seized the opportunity and, along with Lee lieutenant Nick Delucia, took over the running of all of Lee's "rub parlors."

By all accounts, despite Gill's hard demeanor, he had a softer side, along with being very business oriented. He reportedly treated his employees well and lavished his favorites with special gifts. He also required employees to be regularly tested for STDs, which was not the norm in the industry at that time. In 1977, when El Goya, a gay bar in Tampa, Florida, burned down, Gill made arrangements for owner Frank Cocchiara to relocate to Pittsburgh and manage one of his parlors.

But he took a hard line against employees taking advantage of him. Lie detector tests apparently were mandatory for anyone suspected of stealing, whether it was money or something as little as a face cloth.

Barry Paris, Gill's cousin, when talking with reporters writing Gill's obituary, said that Gill could be "intimidating." "But she was personally gentle and nonviolent, and she made a nice corrupt life for herself in a nice corrupt American society," explained Paris.

Gill was married for a time. In late 1977, he married Cynthia Bruno in a civil ceremony in Las Vegas. On the marriage certificate, Gill was listed as "husband," but Bruno apparently retained her maiden name. In 1979, she petitioned the Common Pleas Court to have her last name changed to Gill. According to the *Post-Gazette*, the petition stated that "it would serve

Dante "Tex" Gill's mug shot, 1977. *Pittsburgh Police Department.*

to reduce embarrassment from neighbors, family and friends if your petitioner's name were changed to be the same as the person with whom she resides."

From 1977 to 1984, war existed between Gill and the local mob as Gill tried to carve out his own piece of the illicit trade. The same year he took over Lee's business, the Gemini massage parlor in McKees Rocks was bombed, killing employee Joanne Scott. Later that year, one of Gill's associates, Anthony Pugh, was assassinated in his home. The following year, Delucia and two other men were arrested and charged with conspiring to kill Gill after Gill somehow avoided a sniper attack.

The FBI failed to prove its case, but now Gill and Delucia were at odds and would continue to be for three years. A massage parlor downtown was firebombed in 1980, killing three men who were sleeping on the top floor. Over the next few years, several women involved with Gill's business were murdered or died under mysterious circumstances.

But try as it might, the FBI couldn't prove that Gill or Delucia were doing anything illegal. Gill, for his part, tried to mask his illicit dealings with legitimate fronts, such as Take Me Paint Me, a South Side business that sold unfinished ceramic items wholesale.

In the end, the feds went Al Capone on both Gill and Delucia, with the IRS prosecuting them for tax evasion. Delucia was convicted in 1981 and Gill in 1984. Gill was sentenced to thirteen years in prison, but his sentence was reduced to seven years when he agreed to close his massage parlors and pay a fine. He served less than three years, and after being paroled, he lived out the rest of his life in relative obscurity, dying in 2003.

But even after death, Tex Gill would become the center of a controversy. In 2018, Rupert Sanders and Scarlett Johansson announced that they were going to produce a movie based on Gill's life, called *Rub and Tug*. The announcement was met with disdain and scorn from the transgender community when it discovered that Johansson was slated to play the part of Gill.

The project drew such heat that Johansson pulled out and the project went dormant. In 2020, *Rub and Tug* was resurrected as a potential TV series, written by Our Lady J and produced by New Regency, Dark Castle

Entertainment and Material Pictures. In a news release, Our Lady J said that the project was committed to selecting a transgender actor for the role of Gill.

"Tex's life story is like no other, and the rich landscape of this unexplored moment in time has truly captured my imagination," said Our Lady J. "I couldn't be more excited about the opportunity to write a gangster drama based on such a fascinating and diverse web of queer characters." Cindy Bruno Gill and journalist Brendan Koerner were said to be working as consultants on the project.

As of mid-2023, the project was still listed on the movie website IMDB.com as being in development, although the writer assigned was Gary Spinelli, not Lady J.

Robert R. Lansberry: Why Couldn't He Get His Mail?

Just because you're paranoid doesn't mean they aren't after you.
—Catch-22

Back when "dahntahn" was the center of Pittsburgh's universe, Robert Lansberry was perhaps the most well-known guy in town. He was certainly one of the most visible. Among the shoppers and businesspeople who crowded the streets of the Golden Triangle in the 1970s and '80s, there were few who hadn't seen or at least heard of the homeless Lansberry. He traversed the streets most days, in almost any kind of weather, carrying sandwich boards filled with questions, warnings about government interference in our lives and messages for local and national politicians.

"Why Can't Lansberry Get His Mail" was the most well known of his messages and also the heart of Lansberry's tragic tale. Lansberry, born in Lawrenceville in 1930, lived what most of us would consider a normal life for more than forty years. He grew up in Morningside. After graduating from Peabody High School, he attended Penn State University, where he earned a bachelor's degree in business administration. He enlisted in the U.S. Navy in 1952 and served for four years, becoming an officer.

When he left the navy in 1956, he worked for a few companies before deciding to go into business for himself. He opened a few grocery stores in Plum Borough and bought some rental properties in the East Hills. Along the way, he got married and had three children.

Then, in the early 1970s, things tragically began to go south. He became a consumer advocate because he didn't like the way banks, public utilities and, for some strange reason, the Milk Marketing Board (known as the Milk Commission back then) treated people. Lansberry began to write letters to government officials complaining about nearly everything under the sun. This included various injustices allegedly done to him and others, perhaps during the Korean War, when he was in the navy. He wondered, for example, whether the government had conducted mind control experiments on him back then. He said that he began to hear voices in his head, which he later attributed to what he called "Silent Radio."

In 1974, according to published reports, Lansberry's wife tried to have him committed to a psychiatric hospital for observation. He fought the attempt, and after a hearing, a court declared him sane. But as a result of that, he told *Post-Gazette* reporter Tom Hritz he felt his wife had given up on him so he left his family. However, in an interview for the documentary *Don't Call Me Crazy on the Fourth of July* by Richard Pell, Lansberry says that his wife took the children and left him. "I don't know where they are," he told Pell. Yet another news report stated that his children lived in Florida.

In any case, Lansberry would spend the next twenty-five years living wherever he could find shelter. Sometimes, with his checks from Social Security and the Veterans Administration, he would rent a room somewhere, such as the Edison Hotel on Ninth Street downtown. Other times he would camp out in places like the hillside running down from Mount Washington or under the Second Avenue bridge. South Side, McKees Rocks, Lawrenceville and Stowe Township all at one time or another were listed as neighborhoods of residence for Lansberry.

He secured a mailbox at the downtown Post Office Building in 1977. In 1978, when it was apparent that he wasn't getting any mail at the PO box—because, he maintained, the government was preventing it—he began creating his sandwich boards and taking his messages to the people.

The most often-seen sign, of course, was "Why Can't Lansberry Get His Mail?" or some variation of it. To be fair to the U.S. Postal Service, it wasn't that Lansberry never got any mail. Rather, his argument was that he never received any mail that was of value. Case in point: he claimed that people would tell him they sent him money through the mail, to help him or to aid in his political campaigns. But he never saw a dime, he said.

Along with the mail signs, Lansberry would also sport signs warning about mind control and complaints about various politicians, such as the mayor or—his favorite target—William Coyne, a U.S. congressman from

Robert Lansberry and one of his more detailed sandwich boards. *Wikimedia Commons.*

Oakland from 1981 to 2003. Lansberry ran against Coyne in Democratic primaries twice, and the day after losing to him the second time, Lansberry carried a sign that read, "Election Was Fixed." He also was sentenced to twenty-five days in jail once for carrying an "obscene" sign attacking Coyne. The sign read, "Coyne suks, socks, scuks." (The misspellings didn't matter to the magistrate; obscenity, apparently, is what you make it.)

At least on one occasion, Lansberry sported advertising. In the fall of 1987, he was seen carrying signs touting two CBS talk shows, those of Wil Shriner and Oprah Winfrey. According to a blurb in the *Post-Gazette*, KDKA's creative services director, Art Greenwald, said, "He's the only outdoor advertising space available at a reasonable price." Lansberry wasn't doing it for the cash; the money he would have received instead was donated in his name to the Boy Scouts. "And it's a good diversion for me to take a break from political signs," he said at the time.

In the '80s and early '90s, you might have thought that his job was "professional candidate." In addition to his races against Coyne, he ran for city council almost annually. Once, for a change of pace, he ran in the Democratic primary for clerk of courts against incumbent Jack Kyle.

If you were to speak with Lansberry over the telephone, or in any setting where you couldn't see his face, you would be hard-pressed to reconcile the soft, cadenced voice with the scraggly bearded man, wearing the only clothes he owned underneath awkward sandwich boards, strolling down Fifth Avenue or Smithfield Street under a hot summer sun or on a cold, blustery day. He was articulate and seemingly in possession of all his faculties. In Pell's documentary, the clean-shaven Lansberry is almost unrecognizable as he pleads his case to the camera.

But it was tough not to think that Lansberry was a few bricks shy of a load when he started to talk about mind control and Silent Radio. He claimed that he was part of the 1 percent of the country that has "extrasensory hearing." As he explained to *Pittsburgh Press* reporter Ann Butler in a 1980 interview, "It's not the ability to hear better than other people. It's the ability to pick up special radio messages being transmitted by them." Asked to clarify "them," he said, "The government, the CIA, them. But they'll never completely mind control me because I'm too tough and too smart."

He also told Butler that his mother, who lived in Lawrenceville at the time, also possessed this ability, which is why the two of them didn't get along.

His wandering and living on the streets made him vulnerable to attack. People would mock him, curse at him and occasionally throw things at him. He was beaten by three men in Point State Park in 1977, suffering a concussion. He was hospitalized in 1980, the result of an incident he couldn't quite explain. He told a *Press* reporter that he was attacked the night before Thanksgiving by "unknown assailants" whom he never even saw coming. The incident occurred, he claimed, on West Carson Street near the Duquesne Incline, and it left him with two broken ankles, a dislocated hip and several lacerations on his forehead.

Was he attacked, as he said? Was he hit by a car? (He said his last memory was of stepping onto the curb after crossing Carson Street.) Who knows? Police had no report of the incident, and no one knows how he got to Mercy Hospital.

Lansberry died in 1999 at the age of sixty-nine, in the VA Hospital in Oakland, of pneumonia after a long battle with cancer. His body was cremated and his ashes interred at Indiantown Gap National Cemetery, Lebanon County, Pennsylvania.

In the pantheon of Pittsburgh's colorful characters, Robert Lansberry's story is definitely the saddest. Was he really as crazy as most people believed, or was there some truth to his ramblings about mind control and mail censorship? No one can be sure, but we do know one thing. Several times over the years, he had requested a copy of his FBI file, if there was one. A year or so before he died, the FBI did indeed send him his file. According to Pell, who said in *Don't Call Me Crazy on the Fourth of July* that he has the file in his possession, it was more than 380 pages and went back as far as 1975.

Sophie Masloff: The "Fussy Grandmother" Mayor

Prior to the untimely death of Mayor Richard Caliguiri in 1988, Pittsburgh had never had a Jewish mayor. Nor had it had a female mayor. But on May 6, seven hours after Caliguiri passed away after a yearlong battle with amyloidosis, an incurable blood disorder, Pittsburgh ticked off both boxes when city council president Sophie Masloff was sworn in to succeed him.

Born in the Hill District in 1917, the daughter of Jewish Romanian immigrants, Sophie Friedman Masloff was not the sort of person Pittsburghers in the 1970s would have elected as mayor. In fact, at the time of her appointment, most Democrats considered her to be a placeholder until the next election, in November 1989. They didn't even think she'd seek election; that's why she had been chosen city council president, because they figured she wouldn't use the position as a steppingstone to higher office.

They were wrong. Masloff demonstrated early on that she was not going to merely keep the seat warm for the next mayor. And when the time came, Masloff's was one of the five hats thrown into the ring for the Democratic primary in May 1989. Her main competition, and the considered front-runner in the race, was Frank Lucchino, the Allegheny County controller.

"People underestimated Sophie all the time, and she kind of played it that way," said Joseph Mistick, who served as Masloff's chief of staff. "She was very smart, even though she had no formal higher education. She read constantly, voraciously. And she had street smarts, from growing up in the Hill District with next to nothing. She was a formidable candidate."

When the primary ballots were counted, she had come out on top with 27 percent of the vote. City Controller Tom Murphy garnered 22 percent, and Lucchino finished third with 21 percent. This assured Masloff of the mayoralty, as no Republican was nominated to oppose her in the general election.

Masloff had always been enamored of politics. Even while attending Fifth Avenue High School, she would spend afternoons at the nearby Democratic Party headquarters, stuffing envelopes, running errands, making friends, listening and learning. Less than a year after graduating high school in 1935, she took a job in the Allegheny County Tax Office. She wouldn't leave government service until 1994.

Masloff worked hard, both in her jobs and for the Democratic Party. In 1976, when a city council seat became vacant, the Democrats endorsed her for the position. She would retain it through three election cycles.

When Masloff assumed the role of mayor, the question of whether she would be a leader or a caretaker were answered quickly. Less than two weeks after taking office, Masloff found herself in hot water with the police department when it was discovered that she had met privately with twenty-one detectives from the narcotics division.

Masloff said that she wanted to get input from detectives on drug enforcement without them feeling constrained by the presence of their superiors. "A lot of things the detectives told me would not have been said in front of top brass," she told reporters. "It was a very productive meeting."

An editorial in the *Pittsburgh Press* called the meeting "Masloff's misstep." As for the mayor, she made it clear that she didn't care what people thought. "If I meet with people and the department heads have a problem with that, that's just too bad….If someone wants to talk, I'm certainly going to listen."

Shortly after that, Masloff took on a British industrialist and venture capitalist and managed to wrangle some concessions out of him. Brian Beazer, whose company had purchased Koppers Inc. in a hostile takeover, was sued by the city over the deal. Masloff, for her part, was quoted as saying that she wanted "to scratch [Beazer's] eyes out."

Turns out, she was just kidding, one of the mayor's well-documented attempts at humor over the years. What she wasn't kidding about, however, was her concern that Beazer was going to uproot Koppers from the Pittsburgh soil, a business trend that had become all too disturbing to residents in recent years.

So, Masloff and Beazer squared off in a meeting, during which the mayor got the industrialist to promise not only to try to keep jobs in the area but also to put down some roots of his own by buying a house in the city. Masloff loved Pittsburgh, and she was committed to doing whatever she could to keep it one of the country's most livable cities.

Even in her downtime, she could be formidable. One afternoon, in 1991, Masloff was in her Squirrel Hill apartment when she heard a noise. Going into the hall to investigate—in her "housecoat" no less, according to *Pittsburgh Press* columnist Brian O'Neill—she discovered two men trying to carry a small safe down the stairs. She scared the would-be burglars off, in the process adding to the Masloff legend.

"What I loved about her was that men didn't know how to deal with her," said Beth Caldwell, founder of the Leadership Academy for Women. "She didn't respond like other women, and so they didn't know what to do with her. So, they just stayed out of her way. I thought that was fascinating."

She had her quirks, which endeared her to some and made her the butt of some others' jokes. Most famously, she was known for her own style of malapropisms, which she insisted were always intentional and calculated. She would mispronounce names, particularly names of musicians and musical groups. She was quoted calling the Grateful Dead the "Dreadful Dead," she referred to The Who as "The How" and she once called Bruce Springsteen "Bruce Bedspring." She explained that she used these flubs as a way to break the ice, catch people off-guard or enliven a boring meeting.

However, because she was a woman, Masloff's foibles drew her more attention than they might have done to a man in the same situation. In the male-dominated political world, any attempt to embarrass a woman or put her in her place was grasped at eagerly. So, in 1992, when presidential hopeful Bill Clinton called her and Masloff blew him off by responding, "And this is the Queen of Sheba," it made national news. ("He laughed about it afterwards," she said.)

She developed a standard joke for beginning speeches at functions such as official dinners or fundraising events: "As Henry the Eighth said to each of his wives, 'Don't worry. I won't keep you long.'"

But her desire to call attention to herself was largely limited to those moments when a lighter touch was required. When it came to her real work, Masloff preferred to stay behind the scenes, choosing to focus on the issue itself rather than her role in it. She also surrounded herself with good people, smart people, to give her as much support as possible.

When asked for Masloff's biggest strength, Mistick—who as of 2023 was a law professor at Duquesne University—said, "Her kindness. She was an extraordinarily kind and thoughtful person who considered her constituents, and the hardships they endured day after day, before anything else."

Nowhere was that more evident than during the crippling Allegheny County transit strike in 1992. Although the Transit Authority was under county control, city residents were adversely affected, and Masloff wanted the strike to end. When she said she was going to intervene, no less a power than County Commissioner Tom Foerster told her that it wasn't her place. He accused her of "meddling."

But Masloff was not going to be put off by the bullying Foerster. Her constituents were suffering. And so she put Mistick and others on the job of finding a way to end the strike. To this day, pundits could debate the proper procedure for handling the 1992 strike, but Mistick called Masloff's intervention "one of her finest moments in public life," and not just because her team found a solution.

Sophie Masloff and Kevin Caldwell at a breakfast for Pennsylvania senator Arlen Spector, 2010. *Beth Caldwell.*

"The mayor was driven into work every day by her police bodyguard, as is the custom," said Mistick. "During the strike, she would have them stop and pick up people walking into town and stuff them in her car. Then, after she was dropped off at the office, she would send [her chauffeur] out and basically run a shuttle service."

Meanwhile, Mistick and City Solicitor Jacqueline Morrow worked feverishly to figure out a way to intervene in the strike. The breakthrough came when Mistick remembered a case he had worked on years previously, in which he was able to petition the state Supreme Court to take jurisdiction because of the case's urgent nature. Called a King's Bench jurisdiction, this law is on the books in only a few states, Pennsylvania being one of them. So that's what Masloff did, and the result was, in Mistick's words, "predictable."

"The day we did this, we got three calls from the county, almost simultaneously," Mistick recalled. "Foerster called Sophie, screaming at her. The county solicitor called the city solicitor, screaming at her, and my counterpart called, screaming at me."

But the county's ranting was to no avail. The Supreme Court was unanimous in its ruling that it was indeed Masloff's place, as mayor, to intervene. The court ordered the transit workers back to their jobs.

Pittsburgh in the late '80s and early '90s was a city in financial straits. The Steel City was no longer producing the world's steel, businesses were relocating to other cities and people were exiting the city for the suburbs. Masloff was hard-pressed to find ways to ease the tax burden on, as she put it, "the retired steelworker in Lawrenceville." One of her solutions has turned out to be a boon for the city and the region. She privatized the Pittsburgh Zoo and Aquarium, the National Aviary and Phipps Conservatory.

"We couldn't pay for them, we couldn't keep them up, and we could no longer justify putting the cost of those things on [city taxpayers]," Mistick explained. "That's who was paying for these regional assets, these regional draws. We helped them with the transition financially. We took them off the books, and they were eligible for federal grants, private grants and to do their own fundraising."

In 1993, Masloff decided not to run for a second term. She was seventy-five. Her husband, Jack, a onetime clothing salesman who was Sophie's staunchest supporter, had died two years earlier. And it was questionable whether she had enough party support to have made running for reelection worthwhile. But it would be an interesting exercise to speculate what Sophie Masloff would have been allowed to accomplish had she been a man. Her critics said that she lacked vision. And yet she proved to be remarkably prescient at times. In 1991, she signed into law a bill barring businesses and landlords from discriminating against gays and lesbians, making Pittsburgh a harbinger of what other cities would do in later years.

When she suggested in the early '90s that it was time for the Pittsburgh Pirates and Steelers to have their own stadiums, people laughed at her. Yet less than ten years later, the North Shore was home to two stadiums, PNC Park for the Pirates and Heinz (now Acrisure) Field for the Steelers.

Sophie Masloff may have been a colorful character in her role as mayor, but she was also tougher than she looked and smarter than people gave her credit for.

Author's note: Although there is no doubt Masloff was Pittsburgh's first female mayor, whether she was the first Jewish mayor is apparently in dispute. According to an article in *The Forward*, the national independent Jewish weekly newspaper and website, there may have been a Jewish mayor in Pittsburgh in the 1830s.

Gloria Forouzan, office manager for former mayor William Peduto, told *The Forward* that her research into Pittsburgh's bicentennial uncovered the fact that the mother of Samuel Pettigrew, mayor from 1832 to 1836, was Jewish. According to Jewish law, that would have made him Jewish.

Pettigrew's father, James Pettigrew, was a Scottish immigrant who fought in the Revolutionary War. In 1782, during a victory celebration for President George Washington, Pettigrew and Judith Hart were married in secret by a military chaplain. Miss Hart was the daughter of Myer Hart de Shira, one of the founders of Easton, Pennsylvania.

The ceremony was secret because neither family wanted the marriage to take place. After they were wed, according to Forouzan, they gained the families' acceptance by agreeing to raise any sons as Christians and any daughters in the Jewish faith.

The website JewishGen.org contains an article on the Jewish history of Pittsburgh. The article states, "The first known permanent resident of Pittsburgh to have Jewish Ancestry was Samuel Pettigrew, son of Judith Hart, who settled in the town in 1814 and later served as mayor."

So, Jewish by birth and Christian by faith.

JIMMIE McKay: THE GODFATHER OF "LITTLE CANADA"

Once upon a time, before the turn of the twentieth century, before the areas around the confluence of the three rivers became one governmental unit, the Northside comprised its own city. It went by the name of Allegheny, but there were many who knew it as "Little Canada" because it was a sanctuary for criminals of all sorts. It was a town where the law was flouted and inmates ran the asylum. For example, in an area of only eight square miles, Allegheny boasted 150 brothels; police saw nothing, so long as their hands saw money.

For more than thirty years, the godfather of this enclave was Jimmie McKay. He was a product of his environment, and he learned well how to make the environment work to his advantage.

McKay, the son of Irish immigrants, was a steelworker turned tavern owner whom everyone, it seemed, admired. All manner of blokes were welcome in his bar on the corner of Federal and Robinson Streets, from jewel thieves and grifters to journalists and politicians. Shortly before his death, he told Ray Sprigle, a columnist for the *Pittsburgh Press*, "About the worst thing I ever did was to take pretty literally that business about live and let live. I just never did anything about people who didn't live right. Maybe that was wrong. I don't know."

Of course, the main reason why McKay never tried to "do anything" about his bar patrons is that he was just like them. McKay would hide the ill-gotten gains of the thieves who came to him for help. He had a crew of people whose job it was to vote early and often on Election Day, even if the names they used were those of electors residing in nearby cemeteries. He spent time in jail for shaking down a doctor and helped another criminal break out of one of the world's most notorious prisons. He was about as far from saintly as you could be.

And yet he was an angel to people in need. When the Allegheny and Ohio Rivers flooded their banks—which, back then, was three or four times a year—McKay would marshal an army of men to help business owners move their heavy furniture and equipment to higher floors. The fact that many of those businesses were brothels bothered McKay not a bit. In fact, because pianos were one of the pieces of furniture that had to be moved in those brothels, McKay's motley crew became known as the Piano Movers Association.

McKay was also the chief enforcer of Allegheny's cardinal rule: you don't bite the hand that feeds you. The city was known as Little Canada because police and elected officials there refused to recognize or execute any extradition requests, no matter what governing body had issued them. Criminals were as safe in Allegheny as if they had fled to Canada—as long as they didn't commit any crimes in the city. But if someone robbed a local jeweler, for example, all the businessman had to do was tell McKay what had happened. It wasn't long before the jewels were being returned with apologies from Jimmie, and the offender was given a "message" by Jimmie's boys—usually in the basement of the police station.

But what Jimmie McKay did best, according to newspaper reporters, was tell stories. Journalists loved to hang out at McKay's place because they would hear stories they could hear nowhere else—many of them told by the owner himself. The only cost for hanging out at the bar was to become members of the Piano Movers Association. It was a price they paid willingly.

The most famous of McKay's tales had to be the escape of Eddie Guerin from the infamous Devil's Island, a French penal colony off the coast of French Guiana (now Suriname) in South America. It was a favorite of Jimmy's because he helped engineer the escape.

As described by Richard Gazarik in his book *Wicked Pittsburgh*, Guerin was a career criminal with an unfortunate habit of getting caught. He served time in Western Penitentiary after stealing the payroll of the *Pittsburgh Commercial Gazette*. After he got out, he moved to England, where he was imprisoned after robbing a bank. He escaped that jail and took off for France. But in Paris, he was arrested while trying to rob an American Express office across from a police station. The courts there were far less lenient than the Americans or Brits, and Guerin was sentenced to a life of hard labor on the infamous island.

Mary Ann Churchill Sharpe, a prostitute and grifter known as "Chicago May," came to McKay's bar seeking help for Guerin, who was her lover. The persuasive and charismatic McKay collected enough money from his mates to hatch an escape plan that involved bribing a couple of Devil's Island guards.

And it worked. Guerin and two other inmates made their way to the coast, where a boat was waiting to take them to the South American mainland. Although Guerin reportedly almost died in the jungle, he eventually made it back to Little Canada.

McKay wasn't a well-educated man, but he had street smarts and common sense. In the late 1890s, when reform-minded politicians began cracking down on lawlessness, McKay realized that it might be time to get out of the bar business. He did the smart thing and sold it, although in later years he could still be found there regaling reporters with stories of the old days.

Ah, but what kind of job could a tavern owner who was most comfortable hanging with the less savory elements of Old Allegheny get? Jimmie decided to go "legit." He became a police detective, calling in some favors from the local politicos to sidestep certain rules that might otherwise bar him from the job, such as his criminal past. Then, in 1907, when Pittsburgh annexed Allegheny, McKay transferred to the Allegheny County Detectives Bureau.

Exactly why he chose police work is a matter of conjecture. Perhaps McKay decided that it was time to collect bribes rather than pay them out.

And McKay certainly took his share while on the force. But he and his boss, Assistant Chief of Detectives Ira Berry, eventually lost their jobs and their freedom over this practice.

The man they protected was Dr. H.J. Schireson, a doctor from Detroit whose bona fides were apparently in order—but not his billing methods. Schireson would have patients take off all their clothes in order to receive a full examination. But while he did his doctor thing, an assistant would rifle through the patient's pockets. Miraculously, Schireson's bill usually equaled the amount of money the assistant found on the patient.

Knowing that overzealous cops would on occasion raid the offices of people like Schireson, the good doctor paid Berry and McKay to give him a heads-up when such raids were planned. But the district attorney found out and fired both men. Then he had them arrested, and they were tried and convicted of graft.

McKay served his sentence, and the whole issue became just another story to tell the assembled in his old tavern. And that was how Jimmie McKay was best remembered. When he died in 1944, the headline on his obituary in the *Pittsburgh Press* read, "Yarn-Spinner McKay of Allegheny Dies." Thousands of people attended his funeral mass at St. Peter's Church. This is how *Press* columnist Ray Sprigle memorialized him: "Publican, patron, and protector of thieves, rough and ready politician who shamelessly stole elections, convicted grafter and jail-bird—but withal a kindly and gentle soul who never in all of his life held hatred in his heart for any man—Jimmie was one of the most lovable individuals who ever walked this earth."

KATE SOFFEL: WHAT SHE DID FOR LOVE

Katherine Dietrich Soffel is a rare entry on our list of colorful characters. She is one of only two people on the list to have had a movie made about their lives (not counting documentaries), the other being Nellie Bly. *Mrs. Soffel* came out in 1984, seventy-five years after its titular character's death, and starred Diane Keaton in the title role.

Not that Mrs. Soffel herself would have been thrilled to know about the movie. By all accounts, Kate Soffel would have done anything to change the way the stars had so fatefully aligned for her in 1902, when she helped two convicted murderers to escape from the Allegheny County Jail.

In 1901, Kate Soffel was the wife of Peter J. Soffel, warden of the Allegheny County Jail. She was thirty-four. The Soffels and their four children lived in a house that adjoined the prison. Kate was apparently a kind-hearted soul, always wanting to see the best in everyone. She often spent time with inmates in an attempt to rehabilitate them. And that was how she met the Biddle brothers.

Ed and Jack Biddle were a couple of Canadian thieves on the run. Originally from Ontario, they made their way down to Pittsburgh around New Year's 1901 and went on a crime rampage. A total of twenty-seven burglaries and robberies were believed to have been committed by the Biddles and their companions, who were known to the police as the Chloroform Gang for their method of incapacitating robbery victims. In addition to the Biddles, the gang comprised Frank Dorman, Jennie Seebers and Jessie Bodine.

In the overnight hours of April 12, the group broke into a Mount Washington grocery store to rob it. However, owner Thomas Kahney confronted them, and he was shot and killed.

By this time, police had gathered information that suggested the gang was holed up in a house on Fulton Street in Allegheny. Police inspector Robert Gray and Detective Patrick Fitzgerald made their way to the house and attempted to gain entry. Shots were fired and Fitzgerald was killed. Additional police surrounded the house, and the five occupants gave themselves up.

The trials came swiftly, aided by the fact that Dorman pleaded guilty and testified against the Biddles. On June 15, John Biddle was found guilty, and his brother was convicted six days later. Their request for new trials was denied, and both men were sentenced to death. Subsequent appeals were also denied.

Governor William Alexis Stone scheduled the men to be hanged at the Allegheny County Jail in January. Respecting the wishes of the men not to be hanged together, Stone sentenced Ed to die on January 14 and John on January 16.

History is a bit hazy on exactly why Kate did what she did. She explained later to a reporter for the *Pittsburgh Daily Post* that she had felt pity for the two men and, after speaking with them, became convinced of their innocence. But Ed Biddle was a handsome and somewhat charismatic man, and evidence suggests that Kate fell under Ed's sway.

In any event, Kate had begun formulating a plan to break the two men out of jail. Over the course of two months, Kate smuggled hacksaw blades, guns and ammunition into their cell under her clothing. Apparently, it helped that

The capture of Kate Soffel and the Biddle brothers. *Wikimedia Commons.*

Kate's father, Conrad Dietrich, was a guard at the jail, although there was never any indication that he knew anything about his daughter's subterfuge.

The men may never have had the chance to escape had it not been for an appeal by the Biddles' lawyers, J.F. Burke and Harrison Bock, to the governor on January 10. One of the points in their plea for a stay of execution was the fact that the men's case had not been before the state's board of pardons. The next meeting of the board was set for January 19, days after the Biddles would have been put to death.

Governor Stone decided to grant the men a hearing before the board and pushed back their execution dates to late February. Thus was the stage set for this Greek tragedy. On January 30, the two men made their escape.

According to published reports, at about 4:00 a.m., Ed Biddle called for a guard, claiming that his brother was sick and needed medicine to combat cramps. When the guard approached the cell door—from which the Biddles had already sliced through the bars—Jack Biddle grabbed the guard by the waist, climbed out of the cell and threw the guard over a railing to the ground sixteen feet below. When a second guard came to investigate the noise, Ed

Biddle shot him in the hip. The Biddles then tracked down the third guard on duty, gathered all three men together and locked them in the lower recesses of the jail.

The two men then changed into the guards' street clothes and met Kate Soffel in the prison library. She led them through her house, past her sleeping husband and children, and the three walked out onto Ross Street, where they boarded a streetcar bound for West View. At the end of the trolley line, they walked about a mile to a farm, where they stole a shotgun and a sleigh and headed toward Butler County.

Two hours later, when the new guards on duty discovered the breakout, Warden Soffel was beside himself with embarrassment and anger, realizing that his wife was part of this plot. (After the Biddles were captured, Soffel had no choice but to resign his post, divorce his wife and leave Pittsburgh. He took the couple's children and moved to Canton, Ohio, where he remarried.)

Meanwhile, police were convinced that the Biddles would try to head back to Canada, and Detective Charles "Buck" McGovern pulled together a posse. Figuring the most likely roads the escapees would take, McGovern took his men to Graham Farm in Butler County and waited. A few hours later, the sleigh carrying the two men and Kate Soffel approached.

What happened next depends on whose account you choose to believe. According to the police report, the Biddles stopped the sleigh and came up firing. Police fired back, and the Biddles got the worst of the deal, being knocked out of the sleigh.

However, before Jack Biddle died, he stated that the three runaways shot themselves, opting for suicide rather than be returned to jail and be hanged. Some historians believe that the detectives may have reacted to the Biddles' and Kate's shots as being directed at them and returned fire.

At any rate, what was clear was that Ed Biddle had three bullet wounds, Jack Biddle was "riddled with bullets" and Kate Soffel had shot herself in the left breast.

Jack died early in the evening of February 1, and Ed succumbed to his wounds later that evening. Kate survived her gunshot, as well as a concurrent bout of pneumonia. In the days to come, she too would give conflicting accounts of her reasons for helping the Biddles. She told Miriam Michaelson, a reporter for the *Pittsburgh Daily Post*, that she had helped the brothers out of pity and because she believed them to be innocent of the grocer's murder. (During the trial, the Biddles claimed that another accomplice, still on the lam, had shot the store owner.)

MRS. KATE SOFFEL DIES ALONE AT THE WEST PENN HOSPITAL

THE LATE MRS. KATE SOFFEL.

Kate Soffel's obituary photo, *Pittsburgh Press*. *Newspapers.com*.

She denied being in love with Ed Biddle, but when she was confronted by the fact that a love letter from Ed to her had been found at the scene of the capture, she reacted almost coyly. As per Mrs. Michaelson's report:

> *I asked Mrs. Soffel how she could account for the long letter, written by Ed Biddle to herself, in this morning's papers. She heard of its publication for the first time, and a faint blush stole over her face. She dropped her eyes and for a minute did not speak.*
>
> *"After all I did for these boys," she panted, "you'd think they'd use me better than that? There are some things women never confess."*

Kate Soffel was sentenced to two years in jail. After her release, she tried to tell her story in the form of a play, titled *A Desperate Chance*. But a Western Pennsylvania judge issued an injunction stopping the play from being produced.

Using her maiden name, Katherine Dietrich—and sometimes going by the name of Miller, her brother-in-law's surname—Kate lived as a seamstress in Old Allegheny until her death from typhoid fever in 1909.

Two days after she died, the *Pittsburgh Press* printed a letter to the editor from a woman identified only as "N.C." from Allegheny:

> *Just a word in defense of Katherine Dietrich Soffel. One of the papers stated that she had no particular ailment, but died of complications of diseases. I think it safe to say that hard work killed her. I knew her in a business way only—she sewed for me—in fact, she did not know I knew she was Mrs. Soffel....All she knew was work, work, work. If there was anything she regretted in her life, she atoned for it, and died atoning.*

Edgar Snyder: The Billboard Lawyer

One could argue (no pun intended) that Edgar Snyder was born to be a lawyer. As captain of the debate team at Penn State University, he was a gifted speaker; his mother once told him, "You could talk your way out of a paper bag."

But young Edgar never imagined that he would one day drag the legal profession kicking and screaming into the new millennium with one simple tool: an advertisement. A simple tombstone ad in the *Pittsburgh Press* would end up revolutionizing the legal profession and change forever how law firms attract new clients.

Snyder was born into a family of Polish-Russian immigrants, the youngest of three children. He wanted to be a doctor, like his older brother, "to make my dad proud," and attended Penn State. But his career as a physician ended before it even started, courtesy of Chemistry 101.

"I either failed it or got a D, I can't remember which, and what was said to me in 1959 was, 'What else are you going to do?'" Snyder recalled. "My mother told me to be a lawyer."

So, Snyder went to the University of Pittsburgh for his law degree and began practicing law in 1968, in a fairly new entity, the Allegheny County Public Defender's Office. "I always wanted to help people," Snyder said. "I couldn't help them as a doctor, so I did as a lawyer. Until 1964 or 1965, indigent people weren't entitled to a lawyer. So this was a great opportunity for someone who wanted to be a trial lawyer."

Snyder was part of a very small team; there were only three or four lawyers, he said, to handle all of the defendants who couldn't afford legal counsel. "And I was good at it," he explained. "I was in a courtroom every day for two years. It served a purpose."

It also earned Snyder a good deal of notoriety, as he often represented people whom no one else wanted to help. Not that he had much choice; as a public defender, you took the cases that were assigned to you and tried to provide the best representation possible. And so it was that on October 23, 1969, Snyder and co-counsel Fred Baxter were assigned to represent Stanley B. Hoss Jr.

Stanley Hoss was a convicted rapist who was housed in the county workhouse awaiting sentencing. On September 11, Hoss escaped from the workhouse and managed to evade police for more than a week, until he was recognized by someone who notified police. Hoss stole a yellow Chevrolet Corvette, and several hours later, Verona police officer Joseph Zanella spotted the speeding car and gave chase. Zanella pulled over Hoss at the corner of Allegheny River Boulevard and Plum Street in Oakmont. Zanella got out of his car and was approaching the Corvette when Hoss leaned out of the driver's side window and shot Zanella in the chest. Zanella died at the scene, and Hoss went on the lam for twenty-three more days. He was captured on October 4 in Waterloo, Iowa, but not before he had kidnapped and killed Bel Air, Maryland resident Linda Peugeot and her daughter, Lori Mae.

The trial was, as expected, "hardly the stuff that litigation legends are made of," Snyder noted. Hoss was convicted and sentenced to die in the electric chair, although Snyder did get the death sentence overturned on appeal. But it was a great experience for the young attorney. In the 1970s, he said, "I had the largest criminal practice in Pittsburgh representing homicide defendants."

"I've been a lawyer for 55 years, and that was the most exciting time of my career," Snyder noted of his time as a public defender. "I wanted to get people out of trouble, or at least provide them with some help. That appealed to me. Plus, I learned how to speak legalese in a way that was not legalese, because I had to talk to everyday people and explain their situation."

While Snyder was working in the public defender's office, he also opened a law office in Duquesne, Pennsylvania. He practiced law at night as a "jack of all trades," helping people with everything from personal injury law to real estate.

In 1982, Snyder married a woman who worked as a marketing professional, helping companies and individuals advertise their businesses. At about the same time, two legal decisions would forever change Snyder's practice—along with the entire legal profession. The first was that the U.S. Supreme Court ruled that lawyers could advertise their services.

"They felt, rightfully, that people who had no money were being denied access to legal services," said Snyder. "Personal injury lawyers didn't charge any money to their clients. We took cases on a contingency basis, but people didn't know that."

The second legal happening was that, in Pennsylvania, the law on drunk driving had been changed. The state legislature, wanting to crack down on drunk driving, stiffened the penalties for DUI convictions.

"The law used to be that drunk driving arrests were handled as summary offenses in a magistrate's office," Snyder explained. "If you didn't kill or very seriously injure somebody, you didn't go to jail or even get a criminal record. But now, it could be considered a high-grade misdemeanor or a felony. You could go to jail or lose your license."

Snyder's wife, Sandy, convinced her husband to take advantage of the new laws and advertise his services. So, on May 16, 1983, Snyder took out a small "tombstone" ad in the *Pittsburgh Press*. The ad simply stated:

> *Charged with drunk driving?*
> *Under new PA law, drunk driving*
> *Is a serious offense. Make sure you*
> *Know your rights.*

Below that were listed Snyder's name, his office phone numbers and, most importantly, "Initial Consultation at NO Charge."

The ad was a game-changer. Within a year, Edgar Snyder & Associates had the largest drunk driving practice in the city. He was drawing business from all over Western Pennsylvania. And Snyder made it even easier for people to avail themselves of his services. He retrofitted an Econoline van with a desk and would drive his mobile office to people's homes to meet with them. It reached the point where Snyder began to advertise different services, such as personal injury cases, "because I didn't want to represent drunks for the rest of my life."

But if Snyder felt shocked by the volume of business his newspaper ads generated, he would be overwhelmed by what occurred when he upped the ante.

"Sandy said, 'We really ought to go on television,'" Snyder recalled. The problem was, the cost of television ads in Pittsburgh were out of his still-small firm's budget. So they chose Johnstown, Pennsylvania, to test the TV market, and the result was, "explosive. Phones ringing off the hook." Snyder opened a law office in Johnstown. Then he repeated the story in Altoona and Erie.

"Any place there was a TV station, we opened an office," he said. The firm now had enough money to hit the Pittsburgh market, and it became inundated with business—almost too much business. Snyder's biggest fear became going bankrupt because of mismanaging the business. Slowly, however, he learned how to handle a large volume of cases, and the firm grew "exponentially" every year, to the point that Snyder stopped practicing law and became a business manager.

By now, Edgar Snyder had to be the most celebrated lawyer in Pittsburgh. The toast of the town, fellow barristers lauding him for his foresightedness and trailblazing achievements. Right?

Snyder laughs at that image. "I was a pariah," he said. "I was shunned professionally, the subject of tremendous ridicule. About the nicest things anyone could say to me was, 'What's a nice lawyer like you doing prostituting yourself and becoming an ambulance chaser?' I was told I couldn't join the Cambria County Bar Association; this is what I contended with."

"I loved it," he added. "For five years all they did was criticize me, and nobody competed. I said to myself, give me five more years of people hating me and I can retire in my forties. The more insulting people were, the happier I was inside."

Criticism wasn't all Snyder endured. For three years, his firm was audited by the Internal Revenue Service because 50 percent of his overhead went to advertising. "There was no model for that. The IRS was sure there had

Edgar Snyder, with a cardboard cutout of him in his legendary pose. *Edgar Snyder.*

to be something shady," he explained. "But after three years of turning up nothing, they left me alone."

One of Snyder's most celebrated ads was set in a junkyard. There was a desk set on the ground, with Snyder standing behind it (actually, some fifteen feet away from the desk). The film crew hoisted a junked car on a crane about forty feet in the air, out of view of the camera. Snyder looked into the camera and said, "If you've been in an accident, bring your problem to us," and then the car was dropped onto the desk.

"I can look back on it today and say it was outrageous, but it worked," he said. "It was funny as hell. The ads drove lawyers crazy as being unprofessional. They thought it was schlock, undignified. But the people loved it. I talked with my hands, because that's who I am. People said it made them think I was talking right to them."

Television gave Snyder exposure and name recognition unparalleled in the industry. A poll of residents in Blair and Cambria Counties, conducted for Edgar Snyder & Associates, showed that Snyder had 99 percent name recognition in the area. By contrast, George H.W. Bush, then the president of the United States, had 96 percent name recognition.

"Imagine that, being more well known than the president," Snyder marveled. "People ask me, 'Isn't it intrusive that you can't walk down the street anywhere in Western Pennsylvania without people pointing at you or stopping you and asking if they can ask you a question?' I say, 'It's not intrusion, it's validation.'"

Finally, he noted, the Allegheny County Bar Association waved the white flag. Snyder was asked to run a seminar for lawyers on how to conduct an advertising campaign. Snyder also helped to set up advertising guidelines to regulate the practice.

After the turn of the millennium, Snyder turned to billboards to continue spreading his message. "Billboards are not the way to build a campaign," he said, in explaining why he didn't use billboards sooner. "It's the way to enhance a campaign. You show people, and keep the name recognition before them."

Snyder retired in 2013 and sold the firm to his law partners. Today, at age eighty-two, he relaxes in his condo in Florida and does the occasional commercial for the firm. His biggest joy today? Giving away money. "My success has allowed me to be philanthropic," he said with pride. "Without that platform to be successful, I could never have done what I do today. That has been as rewarding for me as anything else."

DR. CYRIL H. WECHT:
THE NATION'S MEDICAL EXAMINER

If Cyril Wecht had pursued a career in music, few people could have faulted him. After all, when he started taking violin lessons at the age of eight, he attacked the instrument with a passion that bordered on obsession. He practiced four hours a day during the week and six hours a day on weekends. He was concertmaster (lead violinist) for the orchestra at Fifth Avenue High School, from which he graduated in 1948, for four years. Then he was concertmaster for the University of Pittsburgh's orchestra for another four years while he pursued his undergraduate studies.

But there was never any doubt that Cyril Wecht would one day have an "MD" attached to his name. There was no other career path he could have chosen.

"My father told me from the time I was a baby that I was going to be a doctor," Dr. Wecht recalled as he was on the cusp of his ninetieth birthday. "It was the dream and wish of Jewish immigrant parents. I never thought otherwise. I was an obedient only child."

Wecht is also an overachiever of the highest order; his *curriculum vitae* is thirty-three pages long. So it should be no surprise to learn that Wecht is not only a doctor. He's also a lawyer, having law degrees from both Pitt and the University of Maryland. That combination makes Wecht perfectly suited to his chosen profession, forensic pathology. The knowledge of both the medical and legal aspects of criminal and civil investigations involving death have made him perhaps the most sought-after medical examiner in the world. Of course, being a central figure in one of the most controversial homicide investigations in U.S. history, the President John F. Kennedy assassination in 1963, certainly didn't hurt.

Wecht was born in 1931 in the village of Bobtown, in Greene County near the West Virginia border. He was the lone child of Nathan, a Lithuanian shopkeeper, and his wife, Fannie, a Ukrainian immigrant. When Cyril was young, the Wechts settled in Pittsburgh's Hill District, where Nathan ran a grocery store.

After graduating as valedictorian of his class at Fifth Avenue, Wecht went up the street to Pitt, where his seemingly boundless energy—and a fair amount of charisma—made him an active and popular undergrad. During his first four years, in addition to being concertmaster, Wecht was president of Student Congress; president of his fraternity, Phi Epsilon Pi; vice-president of and varsity debater for Pitt's debate team; business manager for the Pitt

Dr. Cyril Wecht, 2020.
Wikimedia Commons.

News and the Pitt Players; and, despite being Jewish, president of the Pitt YMCA. It seemed that whatever Wecht set out to do, he excelled.

"In my senior year, I was making my usual pitch for the selling of group tickets [for the Pitt Players], and Professor Harvey Pope, who was the theatrical director at Pitt, asked me to read for him," Wecht said. The upshot? Pope gave Wecht the coveted role of the stage manager in Thornton Wilder's *Our Town*.

During Wecht's undergrad years, there were some students who believed that Wecht was actually pre-law rather than pre-med. That idea buried itself in Wecht's brain, only to resurface during his third year of med school.

"The first two years of medical school are pretty rough," Wecht said. "In my third year I contacted the AMA, and they put me in touch with a doctor-lawyer who invited me to a national conference in New York City. That gave me information of a more substantive nature than I had been able to acquire about the profession previously. I made up my mind I was going to get a law degree, and it became quite apparent that the interface of law and medicine is undoubtedly forensic pathology by the nature of what we do."

Now, finally, Wecht's career path was set. He applied for a residency in pathology at the Veterans Administration Hospital in Oakland. At the same time, he asked for permission to attend law school—while doing his residency. Despite the double workload, Wecht made the *Pitt Law Review* and caught the eye of the U.S. military. Wecht had previously been drafted but had received a college deferment.

"I wanted another year deferment, but the military felt I was ready to serve as a pathologist," Wecht said. "They didn't care about law school." Wecht served as a captain in the U.S. Air Force for two years at Maxwell AFB in Montgomery, Alabama, home of the largest air force hospital in the country.

After his service, Wecht needed one more year of residency and another year of law school to satisfy the requirements of both disciplines. "I looked around and saw that the setup was perfect in Baltimore, so I applied and was accepted as a research fellow in forensic pathology and associate pathologist in the office of the chief medical examiner of Maryland and was accepted at the University of Maryland Law School."

Wecht did his fellowship during the day and attended law school in the evening, and by the summer of 1962, he had everything he needed to return home and set up shop. Wecht had accomplished in five years what might have ordinarily taken twice as long. (For the record, his family appears to be just as motivated and driven as the patriarch. Wecht's wife, Sigrid, has earned three degrees. And the couple's four children all hold degrees from Ivy League schools: David is an Allegheny County Common Pleas Court judge, Dan is a neurosurgeon, Ingrid is an OB/GYN doctor and Benjamin is a writer who has coauthored two books with his father.)

He set up a private practice, Cyril H. Wecht and Pathology Associates, and became head of pathology at St. Francis Hospital. He also served as assistant district attorney and medical advisor to the Allegheny County District Attorney's Office. In 1965, he became deputy coroner of Allegheny County. Four years later, he was elected coroner, a position he would hold until 1980. It was during his time with the district attorney's office that he would give the speech that would elevate his profile, cement his legacy and become Wecht's first controversy.

"Charlie [McInerney, head of the DA office's "crime lab"] asked me if I would like to speak at the American Academy of Forensic Sciences meeting in February 1965," Wecht related. (The AAFS is the largest and most prestigious organization of its kind in the world.) "It was to be a plenary session on the Warren Commission Report."

Had McInerney not invited Wecht to speak at the AAFS conference, would Wecht have ever picked up the Warren Report? As Wecht pointed out, the report is twenty-six volumes long—with no index. But Wecht, as dedicated to his profession as he is, may have one day decided to dive into the tome whether or not he was required to.

But fate decreed that he would delve into the minutiae of the voluminous report in 1964, and the wheels of controversy were set in motion. After detailed study of the report, Wecht discovered that he disagreed with the commission's findings. The Warren Report concluded that Lee Harvey Oswald had acted alone. He fired three bullets from his sixth-floor perch in the Dallas Book Depository. One shot missed, one struck both Kennedy and Texas governor John Connally and the third hit the president in the back of the head, killing him.

However, Wecht believes that the nonfatal injuries to Kennedy and Connally were caused by more than one bullet and that those bullets came from different directions. He would spend the next seven years arguing his case, all the while trying to gain access to evidence that would, he believed, settle the matter.

The evidence was being housed in the National Archives in Washington, D.C., having been donated by Jacqueline Kennedy in 1966 with one proviso: the materials were not to be seen by the public for seventy-five years. The only exception made was that, after five years, "recognized authorities in the field of forensic pathology could apply to examine them."

In August 1972, Wecht became the first such professional to gain access to the materials. What he saw was underwhelming, to say the least. It was what he *didn't* see that would make headlines in the *New York Times* on August 27.

"Mystery Cloaks Fate of Brain of Kennedy" was the title of writer Fred P. Graham's article, the result of an exclusive interview with Wecht. The pathologist expected to be able to examine the late president's brain, which reportedly had been preserved in formalin, along with microscope slides of tissue removed from Kennedy's wounds.

The whereabouts of the president's brain and the slides have never been revealed. According to the *Times* article, the Justice Department never requested those items for the archives because, in the words of Kennedy spokesperson Burke Marshall, "they have no bearing on who killed the President." Other critics of Wecht accused the pathologist of grasping at straws because the evidence in the archives didn't prove his theory.

"Most of the unpleasant reactions came from members of the federal government or supporters of the Warren Commission," Wecht said. "From others I have received praise, admiration and respect."

Wecht has since written scores of articles regarding the assassination and subsequent investigation, as well as a book titled *Into Evidence: Truth, Lies and Unresolved Mysteries in the Murder of JFK*. He also has testified under oath three separate times about the JFK assassination.

The Warren Commission critique put Wecht into the spotlight, but it was only the first of many high-profile cases the pathologist would be called on to consult. The list of people with whose cases he has been involved reads like a who's who of death in the late 1900s: Robert F. Kennedy, Sharon Tate, Brian Jones, Elvis Presley, Kurt Cobain, JonBenét Ramsey, Dr. Herman Tarnower, Sunny von Bulow, Vincent Foster, Laci Peterson and both Anna Nicole Smith and her son David. In all, Wecht has performed more than fourteen thousand autopsies.

It was inevitable that Wecht, working for the government as he did in the early '60s, would become involved with politics. After he was elected coroner of Allegheny County in 1969, he threw himself wholeheartedly into the political arena and would remain a force in county politics off and on until 2006—but not without his share of controversy.

Over the course of forty years, Wecht would serve as county coroner twice, from 1970 to 1980 and from 1996 to 2006. He was elected chairman of the Allegheny County Democratic Party in 1978, and the following year he became an Allegheny County commissioner. He also ran unsuccessfully for the U.S. Senate in 1982 and was defeated in a bid for reelection to the county board of commissioners. After failing to gain the chairmanship of the Pennsylvania Democratic Party in 1983, he stepped back from politics until he ran for coroner in 1995.

During his tenure as coroner, Wecht was indicted twice, once by Allegheny County and once by the federal government. In 1979, the coroner was accused of benefiting from his office by using county facilities and equipment for non-county business and profiting from the extra work. During a nearly two-month trial, Wecht was exonerated. However, in a civil action, he eventually agreed to pay the county $200,000 for conducting private business at the county morgue.

In 2008, the federal government brought eighty-four separate charges of public corruption against Wecht. However, it was widely believed that the charges were politically motivated. Roughly half the charges against Wecht were dismissed with prejudice, meaning that the government could not file those actions again. In the ensuing trial, a mistrial was declared after the jury failed to reach a verdict on any of the remaining counts. Although the government wanted to retry the case, there was so much heat coming from several sources alleging "selective prosecution" that all charges were dismissed a year later.

And now (Wecht is ninety-two as of this writing), twenty-five years or more after most people have retired, he continues to plug along, working cases in either an active or consulting role. The day before he was interviewed for this profile in 2020, Wecht performed four autopsies—one of them a fourteen-year-old Native American girl, exhumed in Montana and delivered to Wecht.

The obvious question, then, becomes "Why?" "The answer is very simple," Wecht said. "What field of endeavor is there that is more exciting, gives you the opportunity to deal with doctors, lawyers, judges, government agencies, social workers, law enforcement and then, at the academic level, people in high school, college and the post-graduate level. What could be more exciting, more challenging, more intellectually demanding and of more significance or of greater pragmatic importance?"

"I think about retirement," he added, "but how many books can you read, how many movies can you see? What the hell else am I going to do?"

Part II
ARTS AND ENTERTAINMENT

Bill Cardille: "Chilly Billy"

Meteorologist. DJ. Sports announcer. Movie host. Character actor. Telethon promoter. Commercial pitchman. Travel agent.

From the 1950s to the early part of the new millennium, these descriptors all applied to one man in Pittsburgh: William Robert Cardille. At one time or another, Bill Cardille assumed one or more of these roles.

Cardille's two most memorable jobs, of course, are as the announcer for *Studio Wrestling* in the '60s and '70s and, later, as the host of *Chiller Theater*. However, he actually got his start as a radio DJ, in 1951, at station WDAD in Indiana, Pennsylvania. But he was there at the beginning for WIIC-TV; his was actually the first voice heard on the NBC affiliate when it went on the air on September 1, 1957.

Cardille was a native of Sharon, Pennsylvania, and graduated from Sharon High School in 1947. He studied English and speech at Indiana University of Pennsylvania—then known as the State Teachers College at Indiana. He got his start in television in 1952 at WICU in Erie, Pennsylvania.

He was a gifted athlete, lettering in tennis and playing varsity basketball in college. As a matter of fact, when he left for Erie, in addition to an announcement in the *Indiana Gazette* there was this small item in the *Gazette*: "Glenn Sanner of Methodists was the scoring kingpin during first half play in the Church League with 122 points in five games, for a 24.4 average. His closest competition came from Bill Cardille of St. Bernard II, who is now gone from the scene. Cardille accepted a TV staff announcing spot in Erie after scoring 97 points in five games for a 19.4 per game mark."

While in college, Cardille also was the radio announcer for STC football games and was active in drama and music groups.

When he worked at WICU, one of his jobs was to interview professional wrestlers who were touring the area. This was done during the intermissions of live wrestling shows broadcast on the station from the Marigold Gardens in Chicago. Little did Cardille know how much wrestling would play into his future.

In 1959, *Studio Wrestling* debuted on WIIC. The sport was just beginning to become established in Western Pennsylvania, and WIIC fashioned a wrestling arena, seating three hundred, in one of its studios. The program—"90 minutes of organized mayhem"—aired on Saturday evenings at 6:00 p.m. Its host and announcer was Mal Alberts, WIIC's sports director. But Cardille would fill in whenever Alberts was unavailable. So, when Red Donley replaced Alberts as sports director in 1961, Cardille was the logical choice to succeed Alberts.

Cardille was a natural pitchman, and his elevation to announcer came at just the right time for him. Wrestling was becoming so popular that people would line up outside the WIIC studios at noon on Saturdays to land one of the three hundred tickets given out each week. He was aided, independently, by two other characters. One was local wrestling legend Bruno Sammartino, and the other was a feisty middle-aged lady named Anna Buckalew—or, as Cardille began calling her, "Ringside Rosie." (Interesting sidelight: When Cardille came to WIIC, the studio was still under construction. According to the website chillertheatermemories.com, one of the carpenters working at the site was Sammartino.)

Cardille was an excellent announcer—and would be a rarity today because he knew when to talk and when to be quiet. Frank Holtz, a local wrestler known as the Fighting Cop from Carnegie, explained Cardille's style to *Post-Gazette* sportswriter Mark Madden: "He knew how to highlight people who weren't that interesting and how to explain what was happening so that anyone could understand it."

Cardille announced for *Studio Wrestling* on WIIC until 1972, when station executives decided that the station should be more news-focused to compete with the other network affiliates, and 6:00 p.m. was considered a news slot. (It was once reported that *Studio Wrestling* was so popular that Bill Burns, perhaps the most famous of Pittsburgh's newscasters and an icon at KDKA, started taking weekends off so he wouldn't be on air at the same time as wrestling.)

Cardille took the loss in stride. After all, he still had another gig at the station, and it would become a bigger deal than *Studio Wrestling*. It was Chiller Theater, and it earned Cardille the moniker he would take to his grave: "Chilly Billy."

Chiller Theater began as a Saturday afternoon movie show in 1964, airing mostly B horror and sci-fi movies. Cardille hosted the show in a black suit and tie, with a mad scientist's laboratory as his set. In addition to announcing each week's movie, he created skits with a variety of "interesting" people that he would stage during commercial breaks.

Chiller Theater was a hit right out of the gate. In less than four months, it would be moved to Saturday nights at 11:30 p.m., following the nightly news. It became a double feature as well. *Chiller Theater* would hold that time slot for sixteen years, remaining so popular that in 1975, when NBC created *Saturday Night Live*, WIIC refused to air it. For the first four years of its existence, *SNL* was picked up by WTAE, the ABC affiliate in Pittsburgh.

Cardille was definitely the reason for *Chiller Theater*'s success. He never allowed the show to stagnate. Over time, his look changed, from the staid suit and tie to a tuxedo and ruffled shirt. The laboratory set was swapped out for a Transylvanian-like castle, and his cast of zanies became more colorful— and more regular. Cardille referred to them as the Chiller family, and they included Norman the Castle Keeper, Stefan the Castle Prankster, Georgette the Fudgemaker and the lovely yet silent Terminal Stare. Sometimes it was hard to tell which were cheesier, the movies or Cardille's skits. But that was part of the charm of the show, and viewers loved it.

Still, it was only a matter of time before station management caved into the network pressure to bring *SNL* into the fold. It was a smash in its own right, and after the 1979 season, WIIC decided to air *SNL* and push *Chiller Theater* to a 1:00 a.m. slot. Ratings began to decline, and a decision to push the show back by another hour was its death knell. The last *Chiller Theater* aired on January 1, 1984.

Cardille would continue to work in various capacities at WIIC until his retirement from television in 1998. For some time, he was the weatherman for the morning and noontime newscasts. And every Labor Day weekend, he was the local host of the annual Jerry Lewis Muscular Dystrophy Association Telethon.

But his broadcast activities weren't limited to Channel 11. He also did the play-by-play of WPIAL basketball playoff games on WQED-TV. He hosted morning radio programs on stations WWSW and WIXZ. And after he retired from WIIC, he took over the midday slot at WJAS radio, from which he retired in 2014.

Cardille also appeared in a few movies, courtesy of George Romero, a fellow Pittsburgher who once said he got his desire to make horror films from watching *Chiller Theater*. Romero cast Cardille as a news reporter in the 1968 cult classic *Night of the Living Dead*, which Romero wrote and directed. He also appeared as a TV interviewer in the 1990 remake, and he was uncredited as a zombie wandering Monroeville Mall in *Dawn of the Dead*. (Romero's third zombie movie, 1985's *Day of the Dead*, starred Cardille's daughter, Lori.)

In 2010, Pittsburgh, Sharon, Allegheny County and Mercer County all declared September 28 Bill Cardille Day in honor of his achievements and longevity in TV and radio. He received numerous other awards in his lifetime, including being inducted into the Pennsylvania Broadcasting Hall of Fame and the AFTRA Hall of Fame. Several organizations named him their Man of the Year at one time or another.

Bill Cardille passed away in 2016, of cancer, at the age of eighty-seven.

PORKY CHEDWICK: THE PLATTER-PUSHIN' PAPA

Porky Chedwick was known by many names in his lifetime, most of which he himself created. To thousands and thousands of local teenagers in the 1950s through the '80s, he was the Daddio of the Raddio, Pork the Tork, the Boss Hoss with the Hot Sauce and the Pied Piper of Platter. He was the radio DJ the "cool kids" listened to and the man musical artists and their agents turned to when they thought their record had potential. He was an astute judge of what his listeners wanted to hear, and not only was he perhaps the most colorful character on radio, he was also one of the most color-blind. Scores of musical groups, both white and Black, owed their success in part to Porky Chedwick.

He was born George Jacob Chedwick in 1918 in Homestead, Pennsylvania, the second of ten children. Nicknamed "Porky" by his mother, Chedwick was often a babysitter for his younger siblings. In the summertime, that usually meant keeping an eye on the neighborhood's children as well. Chedwick would take this responsibility so seriously that it would morph into a lifetime of helping young people stay on the straight and narrow.

Growing up, Chedwick's main passion was sports. Because of some medical issues—for instance, his eye was badly damaged by an errant slingshot when he was only eight—Chedwick wasn't an athlete. But he followed sports. He would announce sporting events at Munhall High School, the school from which he graduated in 1936, and one of his first jobs was as a sports stringer

Porky Chedwick at the Attic Record Store, Squirrel Hill. *Travis Klein.*

for the *Daily Messenger*. By then, he was known as Craig, the first name he gave himself. At the age of twenty, a brief in the *Pittsburgh Post-Gazette* noted that Chedwick had amassed "one of the finest" collection of sports articles and photographs in the country.

Chedwick got a late start into his radio career, at the age of thirty. When station WHOD went on the air in Homestead on August 1, 1948, for the first time, Chedwick was there—but not, technically, as a disc jockey. He started out with a sports and music show on WHOD, which was billed as the "Station of Nations," designed to serve the diverse local population of European immigrants. For the next four years, that would be primarily how he was known, as a sports announcer.

Even in that role, he demonstrated the "out of the box" thinking that would carry him to music fame. For example, in October 1948, during the World Series between the Boston Braves and the Cleveland Indians, Braves outfielder Jim Russell was hospitalized in Pittsburgh with what turned out to be a career-ending heart ailment. (Russell was a native of Fayette City in nearby Fayette County, Pennsylvania.) According to the *Post-Gazette*, Chedwick did what no other sports announcer thought to do: he brought his radio equipment down to Mercy Hospital and conducted a bedside interview with the thirty-year-old ballplayer.

But Chedwick also was passionate about music, and he began to attract listeners who liked his platter patter as much as others enjoyed his sports talk. Gradually, the station gave him more time to play music, and Chedwick chose genres he enjoyed, mostly blues and jazz. The records he spun were the same that he had used for years at the record hops he had been playing in the more integrated parts of Pittsburgh and its suburbs. He knew what he liked, and he knew what listeners would respond to. By the fall of 1952, he had shed the sports side of his job and emerged as a full-time DJ.

"Porky Chedwick at WHOD is the latest disc jockey to catch on," read a brief in the *Post-Gazette* in September 1952. "Porky's been an announcer at the station for three years, but a platter spinner for only three months and his mail has been on the terrific side."

Indeed, his style was unique, according to Travis Klein, president of the Pittsburgh Music Hall of Fame, who first met Chedwick when Klein was a young man working at Itzy Klein's Record Store in the Hill District. Itzy Klein was a record wholesaler and retailer who sold the kind of music Chedwick liked and wanted to play. "It was the way Porky talked," Klein explained. "There probably wasn't any other 'personality' DJs when he was on the air. He had a rap, and that was pretty special because nobody else was doing that."

But Chedwick really didn't have much choice. WHOD had one thousand watts of power; by contrast, KDKA radio sported fifty thousand watts of broadcasting juice. So Porky knew he had to distinguish himself to make his style unique enough that people would talk about it and generate more fans.

An example of what Klein was talking about can be found on the profile of Porky done by the Pittsburgh Music History website:

> *I'm not a Spaniard, I'm not from Spain.*
> *I'm Pork the Tork and I'll fry your brain!*
> *I've got more lines than Bell Telephone.*
> *I've got more jams than Smuckers.*
> *I've got more moves than Allied Vans.*

"Wolfman Jack and Alan Freed and others, he was playing R&B before they were," Klein said. "And he played the oldies, but he played a different kind of oldie than anyone else around the country. Instead of mainstream groups, he played some jazz, instrumental, gospel, blues, solo artists. He also flipped over records. He'd play the B side."

Chedwick was under no obligation to play a particular record, or a certain side, for that matter. So he played what he thought his listeners would most enjoy. "If Porky played a record, he had an audience who could turn that record into a hit," Klein explained.

Black musicians and their representatives also loved Porky because they could get airtime with him at a time when many mainstream stations refused to play their music. As a matter of fact, many parents apparently thought that Porky Chedwick himself was black. When they discovered otherwise, there was a huge outcry from adults who thought that Chedwick's goal was to corrupt their children.

Nothing could have been further from the truth. Chedwick always lived a Christian lifestyle; he didn't drink and he didn't smoke. If he had a vice, Klein said, it was that "supposedly he was a skirt chaser in his early days." And few celebrities did more to help kids stay in school, stay active and stay out of gangs than Chedwick—a fact noted by no less an influencer than Estes Kefauver, the conservative senator from Tennessee who in 1955 commended Chedwick on the floor of the U.S. Senate for his efforts to fight juvenile delinquency. And Porky's care and concern and sense of fair play didn't extend only to children or white people.

"Porky was a civil rights activist who preceded the civil rights movement by at least ten years," Klein noted. "He wouldn't appear at segregated events. He played Black music for white people five years before anybody else did. He didn't have an ounce of hate in his heart."

There was another, simpler reason musical groups loved Porky, Klein said, and it was that the influence Chedwick had on his fans could not be overstated. Perhaps the most amazing example of this occurred in the summer of 1961, when the management of the Stanley Theater in downtown Pittsburgh asked Porky to do a live broadcast from outside the theater to promote the movie *Birdman of Alcatraz*, starring Burt Lancaster. The publicity stunt was a disaster because so many people wanted to see Chedwick in person that the flow of fans turned downtown into a parking lot. Not only roads but also bridges leading into the city were at a standstill. Mayor Joseph Barr somehow made his way from his office on Grant Street to Seventh Avenue to beg Chedwick to stop the broadcast. Police estimated that before all was said and done, more than fifty thousand people had descended on downtown Pittsburgh.

Thousands more were stuck on city buses. One of them, a thirteen-year-old named Jeanie, was undoubtedly disappointed that she didn't get to see Porky that day. But she eventually would get to meet the Bossman, and when she did, she made it count. She married Chedwick in 1990 and remained by his side until his death in 2014. Several of Chedwick's friends, including Travis Klein, believe that Jeanie was the best thing to happen to the ever-trusting Chedwick. She became his manager and protected him from anyone who tried to take advantage of Porky's generous nature. At Chedwick's funeral, Klein suggested that Jeanie "added 25 years to his life."

By 1956, Chedwick was the hottest thing in Pittsburgh. *Esquire* magazine named him Pittsburgh's No. 1 DJ, and he held the coveted 4:00 p.m. to sign-off spot at WAMO, the new call letters of WHOD after it was sold that year. He worked at WAMO until 1984, when the station let him go, and then returned in 1992 at the behest of WAMO's parent company, Sheridan Broadcasting.

In addition to his radio show, Porky made myriad public appearances over the years. It is estimated that he hosted or emceed eight thousand music shows and dances. Perhaps the most noteworthy of them was in 1962, when Chedwick took over the new Civic Arena on May 11 for the Porky Chedwick Groove Spectacular. The list of performers was a testament to what the music industry thought of him: twenty-two acts that included Jackie Wilson, Bo Diddley, The Flamingos, The Five Satins, Patti Labelle, Bobby Vinton and The Drifters. The all-day show drew thirteen thousand fans.

Chedwick performed on air at various radio stations in Pittsburgh, even spending some time on internet radio for a few years before in death on March 2, 2014. His last public appearance was at the Roots of Rock-and-Roll concert in Pittsburgh, and it was fitting, because you could argue that Porky Chedwick was the bedrock that secured those roots nearly seventy years earlier.

Vic Cianca: The Dancing Cop

To his fellow officers, Vic Cianca was known as "Gloves." *Pittsburgh Press* columnist Phil Musick once called him the "Nureyev of the Intersection." Most Pittsburghers knew him as the Dancing Cop.

But for more than thirty years, Cianca could be found on busy Pittsburgh streets, using those white-gloved hands and distinctive movements to direct cars, trucks, buses, streetcars and pedestrians safely through intersections at the height of rush hour or at special events.

Over the years, his unusual style would earn him the admiration of Yinzers, the fame of national exposure and the ire of some of his superiors—and fellow officers—with the Pittsburgh Police Department. "I've gotten more guff from the guys I work with than I ever got from the public," Cianca was once quoted as saying. But he endured it all with a smile and the humility of someone who was just doing his job the best way he knew how.

Cianca's style was not unique—you can find YouTube videos of a cop in Alliance, Ohio, from the 1960s known as The Matador, as well as a Providence, Rhode Island traffic officer from the early 2000s, also known as the Dancing Cop. But Vic was one-of-a-kind for this bustling metropolis back in the day, and it brought him into the sights of what might be called the grandfather of reality TV, *Candid Camera*.

Candid Camera was a comedic reality show that caught people in unusual situations—sometimes predicaments created by the *Candid Camera* people themselves. Created by Allen Funt in 1948, the show's staged vignettes always ended with the embarrassed victims being told to "Smile, you're on *Candid Camera*!" These sketches were interspersed with video clips of people doing funny things or doing ordinary jobs in unusual ways.

And that was how Vic Cianca rose to fame. A one-and-a-half-minute videotape, filmed in secret by *Candid Camera* and set to an instrumental of the song "Let's Twist Again," by Chubby Checker, aired on the show December 13, 1964. Cianca was an immediate sensation from coast to coast. A few months later, when fans of *Candid Camera* voted for the best segments in the show's history, the Dancing Cop was chosen second most popular. Suddenly, there was one place where Cianca was most definitely *not* popular, and that was within his own department. Cianca's balletic display, which had gone unremarked on by his superiors for a decade, suddenly was problematic. So, when Cianca was invited to come to New York City to accept a modest award on behalf of the CBS network, his boss said no.

On May 20, 1965, it became publicly known that Superintendent James W. Slusser had told Cianca not only that he would not be allowed to travel and accept his award but also that he would have to stop his expressive movements and conform to a more traditional style of directing traffic. To the media, Slusser said, if his now-famous traffic cop wanted to become an actor, "He should take a course at Carnegie Tech" (now Carnegie-Mellon University).

Two days later, amid public outcry, Slusser changed his mind. But the damage was already done. Cianca's request had actually been made weeks earlier and was quietly quashed. The show, which was due to air May 30, had already been taped and could not be redone without great expense to CBS. Still, even in his belated reversal, Slusser made it clear that Cianca must change his ways.

In a statement to the media, Slusser explained, "Pittsburgh police officers are not taught to direct traffic in the unusual manner that Patrolman Cianca does—nor should they be. Our other traffic officers do an equally effective job of moving traffic by more orthodox methods. Patrolman Cianca's method may be amusing but, if followed by all officers, would be confusing."

But Superintendent Slusser's words rang hollow. He never provided any data to demonstrate that Cianca's "method" was dangerous in any way; no increase in the number of traffic accidents/incidents at intersections where Vic plied his trade, no complaints from citizens that they were distracted or confused by his movements or directions. Instead, dozens of people wrote letters to the editors at the city's two daily newspapers to say how much they enjoyed seeing Officer Cianca at his posts. They praised his "ingenuity and originality in getting a very tough job well done" and said that he brought "smiles to the faces of people who have to battle the snarled-up traffic of downtown Pittsburgh."

In fact, you could argue that Slusser inadvertently acknowledged Cianca's professionalism when he stated that "other traffic officers do an equally effective job." In the end, the superintendent said his piece, and the Dancing Cop continued doing what he had always done, in his own style, until his retirement in 1983. That is, except for a brief interlude in 1969.

In September of that year, Cianca and fifty other traffic cops were taken off their intersections and made to walk or drive the streets as beat cops. A statement from the police department indicated that increased crime in the city made it necessary to place more police on the street as deterrents. Cianca was not happy, and he took his displeasure to the media. He asked for help to "tell the public what happened to me and perhaps public sentiment could bring me back."

People began writing letters not only to the newspapers' editors but also to the Department of Public Safety. At the time, Public Safety director James Cortese admitted to getting "a few [letters] here, but in the best interest of the police force, things will have to remain as they are."

And so they did—for all of two months. Then Cianca and four other traffic cops found themselves back at their posts. This time, it was Inspector William McDaniel, of the department's personnel and finance division, who made the announcement, emphasizing that the reversal had nothing to do with Cianca's complaints. "He had requested to be returned to traffic, and his seniority placed him fourth on the list," McDaniel told the *Post-Gazette*. "That's the only reason he's back in traffic."

Whether or not McDaniel was being forthright didn't matter. Cianca was back where he felt he belonged. He once told Roy McHugh, a columnist for the *Pittsburgh Press*, that "God never made a better job." "No light or sign in the world can ever be a substitute for a traffic cop," he said. "Lights and signs, they don't mean a thing to people. A traffic cop can hold 'em or move 'em."

Even if his superiors didn't appreciate Cianca, others did. The *Candid Camera* video was once used by the United States Information Agency to demonstrate to foreign countries an American cop directing traffic. The video, redubbed with Arabic background music and distributed in the Middle East and Africa, was chosen because Cianca showed "humaneness, love of his job and efficient moving of traffic."

Cianca retired in 1983, on his sixty-fifth birthday, but only because of the city's age limit on being a police officer. After Cianca's death in 2010, at the age of ninety-two, his son, Victor Jr., said, "He'd have worked until he was ninety if he could."

But before he stepped away from traffic, he got one last opportunity for the limelight. He portrayed himself for a scene in the movie *Flashdance*, when Jennifer Beals's character tries to emulate his movements while he directed traffic. After retirement, he did work the occasional side gig for private and public organizations that needed a little traffic guidance at events such as antique car shows, county fairs or local parades. Cianca once was even called on to serve as a consultant for a Wrigley chewing gum commercial being shot in Los Angeles. But on the day of the taping, which was to be done in actual traffic, chaos ensued, and the director asked Cianca to step in and actually direct traffic—putting him in the commercial. Relating the episode to Phil Musick, Cianca was quoted as saying, "I was in heaven."

But what about that big award he was supposed to get from CBS and *Candid Camera*? It turned out to be $500 and a camera. The camera he kept. The money he gave to the Police Widows Pension Fund.

Rege Cordic: The Ultimate Drive-Time DJ

One could probably devote a book to the various radio disc jockeys who littered Pittsburgh air waves from the 1940s through the 1990s. Many were colorful in their own right and had their own fans, based usually on the type of music they played.

But there was a special brand of DJ beginning in the 1950s. They were the drive-time DJs. As cars became more affordable and car radios more commonplace, these young men—and let's face it, in the '50s and '60s it was hard to find a female DJ, let alone one working in drive-time—did their shtick during the morning and evening "rush hours" when most drivers were on their way to and from work.

Some of these DJs did more than spin platters, introduce the news and weather and read the occasional commercial. They kept people entertained with comedic skits, bits of trivia and, once in a while, on-air guests such as musicians who'd come to town to stage a concert.

In Pittsburgh, the man who set the standard for drive-time shows was a local product by the name of Rege Cordic. Cordic was born in Hazelwood in 1926 and raised in Squirrel Hill, the son of a railroad worker. He graduated from Central Catholic High School in 1944, but even while a student, he worked as a staff announcer and sometime sportscaster for WWSW-AM.

In 1948, when Dave Tyson, host of the morning show on WWSW, left the station, Cordic and several other announcers auditioned to be his replacement. Cordic got the gig, and being a naturally funny person, he decided to try to inject some humor into his broadcasts. He started out by making jokes about some of the commercials that aired, sometimes mimicking the voices. But, as he once told a reporter, the lightbulb went off in his head the day he slipped in a football score from fictitious East Overshoe University among the legitimate scores. When that didn't land him in trouble—in fact, it was a big hit with the audience—he decided to go big. He gathered together a group of fellow Pittsburghers—including Bob McCully, Sterling Yates, Bob Trow and Karl Hardman—to create characters and write skits for them. And Cordic knew how to pick 'em. Hardman, McCully, Trow and Yates were all tremendous talents and went on to make their own names in the entertainment industry. He called his crew Cordic & Company.

The idea was for the team's characters to show up in the studio to bother Cordic while he was on the air. And they created some doozies. There was Carmen Monoxide, a man who told terrible jokes and who once "ran"

Rege Cordic stops for a photo op during a parade in downtown Pittsburgh in the mid-1950s. *Wikimedia Commons.*

for political office. Louie Adamchevitz, a garbage man of Slavic origin, was a listener favorite. Brunhilda was the happy-go-lucky visitor who was so large that she had to enter the studio through the freight door. The "coach" from East Overshoe University sometimes popped in, always lamenting the fact that his team never won. The show even had aliens, Omicron and Matildacron from Venus, who sometimes brought along Noodnicron from Jupiter.

The list of characters goes on and on, and Cordic played straight man to them all, four hours a day, six days a week. Cordic & Company was so popular that when a Westinghouse executive was in Pittsburgh to evaluate KDKA and make changes, he reportedly ordered management to steal Cordic from WWSW. On Labor Day 1954, Cordic & Company made the move, and with KDKA's fifty thousand watts of broadcasting power, it was able to snare as much as 85 percent of the listeners in its time slot. The show would open and close the same way every day: at 6:00 a.m., to the off-key strains of "Up a Lazy River," Cordic would welcome listeners with, "Hello there, you lovers of fine music you, and welcome to yet another chapter in the day-by-day, week-by-week, true-to-life adventures of Cordic & Company." At 10:00 a.m., he would wish everyone "a ginger peach of a day."

The show was irreverent but never in poor taste, and because these were all Pittsburgh natives making fun of Pittsburgh, nobody was offended. They *got* what Cordic & Company was trying to achieve. Not that Cordic was above making fun of someone else's misfortune. In 1964, after University of Pittsburgh student Fred Williams accidentally drove off the as-yet-uncompleted Fort Duquesne Bridge—then known as the Bridge to Nowhere—Cordic had bumper stickers made up for a fake contest. The stickers read, "Official Entry, Cordic & Company Bridge Leap Contest," and they were plastered on thousands and thousands of cars by Pittsburgh drivers.

But it was all in fun, like the fake ads Cordic and his team created. There was the Crudley White Liner, a car so thin it could be driven on the while line in the middle of a highway. They hawked Mediocre cigarettes, sold in a stainless steel, crush-proof box. But the most famous of them all was Olde Frothingslosh, "the pale stale ale with the foam on the bottom." The creator of this brew, according to the Cordic crew, was Sir Reginald Frothingslosh from Upper Crudney-on-the-Thames. Other tag lines included "a whale of an ale for the pale stale male," "good for what ales you" and "hippity hops make it tops." Cordic urged listeners to "buy it by the case or sick pack," and in 1955, people could. Pittsburgh Brewing Company, makers of Iron City beer, began brewing Olde Frothingslosh during the Christmas holiday season. Because the foam was supposed to be on the bottom, the can were packaged upside down.

Although Cordic & Company wasn't suited for television—listeners' imaginations were a key to its success—the program was almost as difficult to produce as a TV sitcom. Skits were planned and taped ahead of time. The writers would spend almost four hours a day, after Cordic went off the air, writing, editing and taping. Cordic often credited his engineers, Phil Asher at WWSW and Bill Stefan at KDKA, with being the glue that held the show together so seamlessly.

Cordic & Company ran until November 1965. But Cordic, who longed to become an actor and who had experienced the West Coast during his time being stationed there while serving in the U.S. Navy, felt the lights of LA beckoning him. CBS gave him the opportunity to move when it offered him the chance to take over the morning drive-time slot at KNX-AM. He would be replacing another announcer cum actor, Bob Crane, who was leaving to devote his full time to the TV comedy *Hogan's Heroes*.

Cordic did not last long at KNX. The brand of humor that made Pittsburgh drivers reportedly pull off to the side of the road on their way to work, rather than miss the end of one of his skits, was lost on urbane Angelenos. But the move wasn't wasted. Cordic did realize his dream of being an actor, securing roles in dozens of movies and episodes of TV dramas.

His list of credits includes the TV shows *Gunsmoke*, *Kung Fu*, *The Outsider*, *Columbo*, *Barnaby Jones* and *McCloud*. He had roles in a dozen movies, including Woody Allen's *Sleeper*, *The Seven Minutes* and *The Wild Party*. But even people who had never seen him perform knew him by his rich baritone, which could be heard doing voiceovers for scores of TV and radio commercials, as well as some children's cartoons.

Movies also gave Cordic his final connection to Pittsburgh. In the '60s and '70s, Cordic was the host of the WTAE-TV Sunday Afternoon Movie. At first, he flew to Pittsburgh every week to tape the show. Later, he used a studio in Las Vegas to record his intros.

But Southern California was his home until his death in 1999, of cancer. He was buried at Forest Lawn Memorial Park, where his headstone simply reads "Regis John Cordic, 1926–1999."

Randy Gilson: "President" of Randyland

"What you absorb is what you become."

To most people in Pittsburgh who have encountered him, Randy Gilson certainly qualifies as a colorful character. To people who live on the Northside, Randy is a bit of a celebrity. To people in his neighborhood, he is considered to be an icon or an enigma—perhaps a little of both.

If you ask Randy (he prefers not to be called Mr. Gilson) what he is, he will tell you simply and humbly, "I'm just a person. Please don't put me on a pedestal."

But it's hard not to think of him as something special. After all, since moving to the Northside in 1978 at the age of twenty-one, Randy has been a one-man beautification crew. He has adorned the area with street art, cleaned up vacant lots in his neighborhood and in nearby Manchester and generally been a good neighbor and friend to anyone he meets. Since 1982, he is credited with creating dozens of flower and vegetable gardens on those once-vacant spaces. On top of that, he is the proud owner and curator of a piece of property that has become known as Randyland.

Randyland sits at the corner of Arch and Jacksonia Streets, a few blocks up from Allegheny Commons and West Park. Like its creator, Randyland is hard to describe. The brick building itself has been painted a bright yellow. The lower façade of the building and the surrounding courtyard are decorated

Randy Gilson. *Photo by author.*

with a wide variety of objects that Randy has collected. Is Randyland a monument to junk? A tribute to the joys of recycling? A museum of the everyday? An oasis in an urban desert?

"Randyland is a museum of the heart," said Randy. "No brains are allowed." Randy believes that people think too much. He prefers that people "feel" Randyland, rather than think about what it might be.

Labeling Randy Gilson is similarly difficult, and it's best to experience him by pushing aside any preconceived notions. Randy himself explains to people that he is "ADHD and OCD, with a touch of autism, and so I think differently. My mind goes so fast and in so many ways." (Example: Eight minutes into his interview with the author, Randy said, "Hi. I just realized that I never said 'Hi' to you.")

When he was young, he elaborated, some people called him "retarded," which he admits hurt. It's also a label that doesn't seem to fit, if you assume the dictionary definition; "slow" is one gear Randy doesn't seem to possess. "I just have a different kind of intelligence," he says. "I don't understand school stuff."

But that's okay with him because Randy believes that society puts too much emphasis on book learning and not enough on teaching people the skills they need to survive and thrive in this world.

If you believe in God, as Randy very strongly does, after spending an hour or two with him you might be inclined to believe that if God gave Randy less of a brain than others, he compensated for it by expanding the size and power of Randy's heart. The man has love and empathy in abundance.

Randy is a study in self-effacement. He will tell you he knows nothing about art, even as he sits in a workshop surrounded by the colors and shapes of his artistry. He will say that he doesn't know much and then give you a history lesson of the neighborhood. He will use phrases such as "hot diggity dog" and "skedaddle" and then offer a deep philosophical thought about the city of Pittsburgh and its people. ("Pittsburgh of the past was a fertile farmland, bare but ready to harvest people's dreams, if you planted the seed. And that's what people did, and look at it now.")

How Randy got to this point in his life could be considered something of a miracle, given the circumstances surrounding his childhood. He was born in Titusville, Pennsylvania, in 1957, one of six children born to a local minister and the daughter of a dairy farmer. But while Randy was still young, his dad left his mother for another woman. When Randy was nine, his mother packed up their belongings and moved the children to Homestead, Pennsylvania. Randy was excited to move to Homestead because he had learned enough about the Old West to know that "homestead" meant wide-open spaces and lots of land.

He was sorely disappointed to see the reality. But he grew to love his new town. "I'm happy I grew up in Homestead, where nobody had a lot," he recalled. "I'm happy I grew up the way I did because it taught me to appreciate the little things in life."

Those "little things" manifest themselves in the way Randy has conducted himself since he moved to the Northside. A love of beauty, which has caused him to start gardens all over the neighborhood. A sense of order, which led to Randy's cleaning up of the area's vacant lots. A knack for seeing treasure

The entrance to Randyland. *Photo by author.*

in other people's trash, which you experience when you visit Randyland. "I came in with a paint brush and a shovel and a heart," is how he describes his arrival on the North Shore.

Much of what Randy has accomplished here might not have been possible had it not been for his life partner, Mac McDermott, whom he met in the early '90s. Mac and Randy were kindred spirits—each considered to be "different," each with his own challenges. Mac, born David Paul Francis McDermott in Vandergrift in 1958, was a child with special needs who, like Randy, rose above his handicaps. Mac served in the U.S. Navy in the 1970s before becoming a caregiver—fittingly enough, for military personnel at the VA Hospital in Oakland.

"Mac had even worse challenges than I did," Randy explained. "He didn't know how to talk to people. I was not doing good, he was not doing good, but together we shared a life and built this place."

In 1994, the two men discovered that an abandoned building on the corner of Arch and Jacksonia was scheduled to be demolished. The building apparently had had an interesting past. According to Jim Mullin, former owner and operator of Mullins Diner on Progress Street, the building was owned by one-time city councilman Bernard "Baldy" Regan. Mullin said

Photo of Randy with his partner, Mac McDermott. *Randy Gilson.*

Regan ran an after-hours club called the Democratic Club, which was frequented by members of the Pittsburgh Steelers. (Regan was a close friend of the Rooney family.) But that was long past, and now the site was to be razed in the name of progress. Randy, of course, saw value in the old place and was able to borrow $10,000 to purchase the house. The two men worked to convert the house to Randy's vision, and Mac supported that vision the best way he could, by being Randy's emotional support.

Like most art galleries, Randyland draws different emotions from its visitors. Some walk away wondering what this pile of junk is all about. But many people, like Margaretha Didycz, find themselves in awe of the space, and happiness is the feeling most people carry home with them. "It's pretty much impossible to be in a bad mood when you are exploring Randyland," said Didycz, who lives in the North Hills. Her description of the courtyard approximates a glimpse into the mind of Randy Gilson.

"There are so many colors and textures competing for attention that it's hard to focus on one thing for too long," she said. "When you stop to look at one thing, pretty soon something out of the corner of your eye grabs your attention and pulls you in. You can look up, down, and all around and you are just completely immersed in vibrant colors. It really just makes you happy to be there."

In the same vein, it's almost impossible not to like Randy. Not only is he easy to talk with, but he also genuinely seems to care about other people. Didycz said that when her nineteen-year-old son saw Randy in a craft store, he walked over "just to say hi." Twenty minutes later, Brendan and Randy had finished discussing why Brendan was considering switching his college major from engineering to the arts. "It left a big impression on my son that Randy would take that much time to talk with a total stranger," said Didycz.

Mullin said that Randy would frequently eat at his diner, and the two men would sit around discussing the history of the Northside—stories that Randy will readily relate to anyone who asks.

Life has changed dramatically for Randy in recent years. Mac McDermott passed away in 2019 of prostate cancer, and Randy retired from his restaurant job to devote all his time to his art. The sorrow is still palpable in his voice when he talks about Mac, as is the sadness when he discusses some aspects of his early life. And yet he insists that he is happy in his life and wouldn't change a thing.

Well, actually, there is one thing Randy would alter if he could, and he's adamant about it. He would love it if his home/art gallery had a different name. The moniker by which the property is known was not chosen by its owners.

"I didn't call it Randyland! No! I would never have done that!" he said passionately. He lays the blame at the feet of the *City Paper*, which was where he first remembers seeing the name. "I remember thinking that Dolly Parton had just opened Dollywood, and I thought, 'Oh shit! People are going to think Randyland is an amusement park!'" But the name stuck, and over time Randy has come to embrace it, just as the people of Pittsburgh have embraced him.

Ed and Wendy King: Talk Radio Royalty

Talk radio is ubiquitous these days. For those people who still listen to AM/ FM radio, a quick scan of the dial is equally likely to turn up a talk show or music. Some stations, such as KDKA, have a format entirely devoted to news and talk, and satellite radio has many channels where news and conversation rule.

But old-timers will remember when KDKA was mostly music, except for the occasional news feature show. However, for a few hours in the late evening, Ed and Wendy King ruled the airwaves with a unique style of program they called *Party Line*. It was the original "talk radio" show, and it aired six nights a week (except when the Pirates were playing on the West Coast or when a home game had gone into extra innings) for twenty years.

But although *Party Line* could be considered the birth of talk radio, the Ed and Wendy King version was a far cry from the contentious, controversial, occasionally bombastic talk shows from the likes of Rush Limbaugh and Howard Stern.

In 1950, Ed King—who was working as a producer at KDKA, came up with the wild idea for a call-in radio show. Radio interview programs were not new, or rare, but a call-in show had never been tried. The technology wasn't yet available to easily put phone calls on the air, and even if there had been, the Federal Communications Commission had rules about broadcasting and taping telephone calls.

But Ed wasn't proposing to air the calls. Instead, he planned to take the calls and relate the subjects the callers were talking about to the listeners. He said that he wanted the program to be about topics and ideas and not become a soapbox for outrageous callers to commandeer the program.

When asked what the program was going to be about, Ed responded that that was up to the listeners; he would discuss any subject the callers wanted to broach—within reason, of course (no politics, for instance). And by all accounts, Ed could do it too. He was said to have had an encyclopedic brain, could easily recall facts and dates and was well-read on any number of topics.

Ed planned to go it alone. Wendy, who had met and married Ed when the two worked together at a radio station in Indiana, was just going to sit in the studio and keep her husband company while he did his program. But as she once stated in an interview with WQED-TV, "One night, I just started talking. And I kept doing it, for 21 years."

And there is no doubt that *Party Line* would not have been nearly as popular or successful if it hadn't been for the three-way conversations between Ed,

Wendy and whoever was on the telephone. Ed was a seasoned pro behind the microphone, and Wendy had a soft, mellow voice that was perfect for radio. At a time when radio broadcasters "announced," Ed and Wendy "talked" to listeners, and they were perfect together.

In addition to the phone callers, there were tons of letters sent to *Party Line*. Ed and Wendy would encourage them; the couple would provide a different topic each month so that writers could share their stories and experiences, and letters were read on the air.

During a taped interview with WQED-TV in 2005, Wendy took the camera operator up to the attic of her home and showed off the boxes of letters they had saved over the years. After her death, the letters—like all of the audiotapes and radio scripts from the show—were given over to the Duquesne University Archives.

Ed would introduce the program every evening as a "conversational salmagundi"—a veritable smorgasbord of disparate topics; Wendy would chime in with whatever topic the first caller had brought up, and then the show was on. Conversations were interspersed with various games the couple brought on to the show. The most popular of these was the Party Pretzel, the question of the evening. Listeners were invited to call in with their guesses, and anyone with a correct answer would win a small prize.

Even back then, before the days of Yahoo! and Google, the real trick wasn't figuring out the answer. The challenge was being able to get your phone call through. Timing was everything because listeners were using rotary dial telephones, and the technology didn't exist for stacking up phone calls like aircraft over a major airport, taking each one in turn. Night after night, callers would wear their index fingers out spinning the wheel to EX1-1038 (391-1038) and hoping not to get the "fast busy" signal that meant failure. (At least you weren't required to dial an area code back then.) Some people said that the key was to dial the first six digits, then dial the seventh number immediately after a call ended.

Party Pretzel aside, people listened because they loved the format. There was nothing to get irate over, just fun topics like gardening, cooking, movies, books and more. Many an adult, and child, would be lulled to sleep listening to the quiet conversation. And if they missed the answer to the Party Pretzel, that was okay; the *Pittsburgh Press* ran the question and answer in the next day's newspaper. And the combination of KDKA's fifty thousand watts of power and the fact that the show aired at night, when fewer stations were broadcasting, meant that *Party Line* had a far reach. Ed and Wendy would get calls and letters from across the country.

Jack Bogut, a KDKA radio personality who is another of the legends in Pittsburgh broadcasting, once told the *Tribune-Review*, "They were a broadcast phenomenon that shouldn't have worked. But it worked famously because of their personalities. They were just plain good company."

Ed and Wendy's stories converged in 1945, when the two worked together at WOWO radio in Fort Wayne, Indiana. Ed, who grew up in LaCrosse, Wisconsin, became involved with radio at the age of twelve when he convinced a local radio producer to air a radio play he had written. When he was sixteen, he moved to Chicago and became a freelance writer and actor. Eventually, he was hired to work at WOWO—like KDKA a Group W radio station—as a scriptwriter and advertising writer. However, he left the station for a time to serve during World War II in the U.S. Army Air Corps.

Wendy, born Betty Foecht in Ada, Ohio, graduated with a degree in journalism from Ohio Northern University in 1945. In looking for a job, she received two offers. One was for a general assignment reporter at a newspaper, and the other was a position at WOWO. She chose the latter—her job was the same as Ed's had been. When Ed visited the station while on leave, he met Betty, his replacement, and the two fell in love. It was Ed who first called her Wendy because, he said, she reminded him of Wendy in *Peter Pan*, and the name stuck. In 1946, Ed was transferred to KDKA, and naturally, Wendy went with him.

When the duo weren't on the air with *Party Line*, Ed wrote, produced and sometimes did voiceovers for radio documentaries. Wendy served as his researcher. Wendy also did commercials for AAA Tours and later in life became a AAA Tour guide.

Party Line ended abruptly on November 18, 1971, when Ed King died of lung cancer. Wendy said that she couldn't imagine doing the show without her husband and retired from broadcasting. But she remained active with AAA for years as a guide and spokesperson. Up until a week before her death, Wendy lived in the same house in Greentree where she and Ed hosted their annual Christmas "trim-a-tree" parties. She died on December 6, 2015, in St. Clair Hospital at the age of ninety-two.

Both were honored for their radio achievements. The year after Ed's death, the Ed King Award for best radio show was created by the Press Club of Western Pennsylvania. It is given out annually as part of the Press Club's Golden Quill Awards.

In 2010, Wendy was recognized at a New Media Seminar hosted by *TALKERS* magazine in New York City for being the first female radio talk show host.

PITTSBURGH DAD: YOUTUBE'S GREATEST FATHER

One of the city's most colorful characters is actually a character on TV. Well, YouTube, but still…

He is the brainchild of Curt Wootton and Chris Preksta, and because of YouTube he is known around the world as Pittsburgh Dad.

Technically, Pittsburgh Dad is a series of short films, usually three to five minutes long, in which the main character faces situations that are relatable to fathers and/or Pittsburghers. Physically, Pittsburgh Dad is Wootton, born in Fairmont, West Virginia, and raised in Greensburg, Pennsylvania. Spiritually, the character primarily represents Wootton's father, Keith, who was Curt's inspiration. Keith Wootton passed away in 2019.

Preksta, a native of Munhall, is the director; he and Wootton have been collaborating on projects since 2003. In each of those projects, Wootton has been in front of the camera and Preksta behind it.

Pittsburgh Dad was conceived in 2008, during the filming of *Mercury Men*, a short film series (produced for the SyFy Network's website) meant as a throwback to the old TV and movie serials. "It was a grueling challenge to get this whole thing filmed," said Wootton. "We had a minimal budget, and there were constant deadlines. But during downtimes, I used to do these impressions of my father from when I was growing up. Things he would say, like, 'Open a can of pop, you finish the can of pop.' We didn't think too much of it."

Three years later, Wootton was visiting Pittsburgh (he was living in Los Angeles at the time) and talking with Preksta about possible future projects. The conversation eventually came around to cameras, specifically the one on the new iPhone 3 and how good Preksta thought it was.

"We decided to use the camera to shoot video of me impersonating my dad and throw it online, just for fun," Wootton recalled. "We went to Goodwill and bought some 'dad' attire and went back to his apartment and had four or five scenarios with 'Dad.' Not even jokes, just verbatim things we heard from our parents. We added a laugh track, and that made us laugh even more. We thought it was hysterical."

In addition to the laugh track, the duo added a short intro with some jazz piano—"like *All in the Family*." The first one, "Meet Pittsburgh Dad," was forty-five seconds long. The intention was to share the videos with friends and family, nothing more. Of course, what goes on the Internet stays on the Internet and can be seen by anyone. And this was. The response, according to Chris, was "off the charts." Viewers were quickly clamoring for

"Pittsburgh Dad" in his basement bar. *Curt Wootton.*

more. Within two and a half months, Pittsburgh Dad videos had a total of more than 1 million views on YouTube. Wootton decided to move back to Pittsburgh to devote full time to the project.

There are three types of Pittsburgh Dad episodes. The first is a hot topic, or current events, episode. "We did an episode on the [COVID] lockdown," Preksta explained. "We did an episode on home schooling. When Kennywood Park took out the Logjammer, we did an episode the very next day of Dad saying goodbye to the Logjammer."

The second type is the sports episode. Pittsburgh Dad has a reaction to Steelers game each week, win or lose. Pittsburgh Dad has interviewed coaches and athletes and has reacted to Super Bowl and Stanley Cup victories.

"The third type is just family stuff," Preksta said. "There is no shortage of episode ideas here. We know the character so well we can put him in any situation at all, and he will have some kind of take on it."

For example, there is an episode where Pittsburgh Dad is driving around, trying to find a Pizza Hut. He keeps arriving at buildings that look like Pizza Huts but have been converted into other types of businesses. Other episodes capture Dad's reaction to watching shows like *Games of Thrones* or *Stranger Things*.

There is a script written for each episode before taping begins. Then, as they rehearse, Wootton and Preksta tweak the scripts. "Some episodes have zero improv, while others might have 80 percent improv," Preksta said.

Pittsburgh Dad is usually the only character who appears, or at least speaks, on the videos, but that doesn't mean there isn't a cast of thousands— all right, dozens—behind him. After all, Dad has to have a family and neighbors and co-workers.

His wife is Deb. His kids are Mandy, fourteen; Brandon, eight; and Jessica. Mandy has a boyfriend, Andrew (whom, of course, Dad doesn't like), and Brandon's friend Jeffy shows up from time to time. Dad's parents are Pap and Gram, and Linda (Deb's sister) and her husband, Rick, also come into play every so often.

Dad has a next-door neighbor, Thom, who just happens to be from Baltimore and, as such, is a huge Ravens fan. Dad's best friend is Pete, and other people from the community show up occasionally in Dad's commentary.

The characters have been created as the need has arisen. For example, said Preksta, "We needed an antagonist, and so along comes a Ravens fan who lives right next door."

"The main characters are ones we've just mentioned so many times that they are just fully fleshed out in our minds," he continued. "If we were really pressed, we could probably sit here and give a rundown of what these people are like, what type of people they are."

As for the names? "Sometimes they just come randomly while we're filming, a name just pops into our heads," said Wootton. "Sometimes we research for the perfect name, or we think back to people we grew up with."

The characters all are fictional, except for three. Two of them are animals: That Dog (actually Preksta's beagle Sawyer) has been seen in several episodes. The cat, also unnamed, has appeared once.

The only real person besides Wootton to appear on Pittsburgh Dad is a woman from Cincinnati who was caught on tape crying after the 2016 playoff game between the Steelers and Bengals. Wootton and Preksta happened to see the video and later mentioned her in a few episodes involving games between the two teams. But Wootton and Preksta then decided to take things a bit further, actually tracking down the woman and inviting her to appear on two episodes. The first was shot in Pittsburgh Dad's basement bar, and the other was filmed in Cincinnati, with the woman sitting next to Pittsburgh Dad at a game in Paul Brown Stadium. Although she's never been identified in the series, she has achieved celebrity status in Pittsburgh, being praised by Steelers fans for being such a good sport.

The popularity of Pittsburgh Dad—the series had reached the YouTube milestone of 100 million views by 2018—has allowed Wootton and Preksta to make a living off it. You can subscribe to Pittsburgh Dad's YouTube

Preksta, *left*, and Wootton with Steelers head coach Mike Tomlin. *Curt Wootton.*

channel—266,000 subscribers as of this writing—allowing them to monetize the experience.

"At least 50 percent of the views are from different states and countries," said Wootton. "There are a lot of displaced Pittsburghers out there, and there are others who have never been to Pittsburgh. They come mostly for the sports episodes. They like to hear people making fun of other teams."

Several local companies—such as Pittsburgh Brewing Company, Giant Eagle, Eat'n Park, Hoss's Steak and Sea House and even IKEA—have paid to advertise their products on Pittsburgh Dad. And it's likely they get a good return on their investment; typically, episodes receive between 100,000 and 200,000 views. There are T-shirts for sale through Steel City, and Preksta and Wootton have even written a book entitled *Pittsburgh Dad: Everything Your Father Has Said to You.*

Wootton and Preksta are in high demand for personal appearances, not only around the tri-state area but also in places such as Ocean City, Maryland, and Fort Lauderdale, Florida, where a lot of "ex-Pitts" can be found. They have sailed on the annual Steelers cruise to the Caribbean and have been grand marshals for various parades in the Pittsburgh area. In 2012, Mayor Luke Ravenstahl declared October 25 "Pittsburgh Dad Day."

In 2013, Full Pint Brewing released a beer called "3, 2, 1, Win," named after the Pittsburgh Dad catchphrase said at the end of every Steelers win. That same year, Eat'n Park came out with a limited-edition Pittsburgh Dad Smiley Cookie. So it's safe to say that Pittsburgh Dad is considered iconic by many Yinzers.

For Preksta, a graduate of Point Park University and Pittsburgh Filmmakers, making Pittsburgh Dad has him right where he always wanted to be: behind the camera. But Wootton's current career has brought him full circle, in a sense, which he finds amusing. "College is where they tried to rid me of my accent," said Wootton, who majored in theater at West Virginia University. "Taking voice classes, they taught us how to speak a certain way. And yet here I am, making a living off the accent. But doing voices is what I liked to do growing up, so slipping in and out of the dialect is pretty basic for me. Luckily, I kind of blend into the situation."

But Preksta believes that something much more visceral is going on. "Curt won't admit it," Preksta jokes, "but every day he moves closer to becoming the actual character."

GUS KALARIS: A NORTHSIDE INSTITUTION

The longest-standing character on Pittsburgh streets is a diminutive old Greek man by the name of Gus Kalaris. The ninety-year-old Kalaris has been a fixture on the Northside since 1951—longer, actually, when you consider that he started working with his dad at the age of eight, in 1940. Gus Kalaris is the proprietor of a family business called Gus and Yiayia's.

The business is simple: a yellow cart with a rainbow umbrella, from which Kalaris sells flavored ice balls, peanuts and popcorn. But it's everything to Kalaris, and it means tradition and memories to thousands and thousands of Pittsburghers from the Northside and beyond.

With the exception of a few years when he had to move the cart down the road a bit to accommodate construction, Kalaris has been in the same spot, on West Ohio Street, near the tennis courts in Allegheny Commons, ever since he took over the business when his father, George, died—or, as the sign on the cart says, "Since Your Dad Was a Lad." Every year, from May to October, you will find him and a rotating handful of helpers selling their wares to everyone from toddlers to contemporaries—and even the occasional non-human customer.

As for the cart, it's been there since 1917, when a man named Tatso operated

Opposite: Gus Kalaris hard at work creating his ice balls. *Photo by author.*

Above: Model of Kalaris's cart at the Miniature Railroad and Village display in the Carnegie Science Center on the North Side. *Photo by author.*

it. The cart has become an unofficial landmark; in 2021, a miniature replica of it was unveiled to great fanfare at the Miniature Railroad and Village on display at the nearby Carnegie Science Center. It has earned a spot with other such iconic structures as the original Primanti's restaurant, the Kaufmann Building and Forbes Field.

When Kalaris is asked why he still works at age ninety, he gives a very practical answer: "I continue to work because I get Social Security, but it's not enough." But watching him shave those seventy-five-pound blocks of ice—not a task for the weak-armed—and seeing him interact with customers of all ages, it's obvious that he's there also because he couldn't imagine himself being anywhere else. He once told a newspaper reporter that he had already picked out the headstone for his grave, and he wants his epitaph to read, "I'd rather be in the park."

"Other people take their carts where the people are," said Kalaris. "But people come to us. People know us, they know where we are and we've built up a pretty good business."

The history of Gus and Yiayia's is this: Tatso opened the cart in 1917. But in the 1930s, at the height of the Great Depression, Tatso decided that he wanted to return to Greece. He and George Kalaris were friends, attending the same church, Holy Trinity Greek Orthodox Church. So when Tatso made known his plans for leaving, George Kalaris offered to buy the cart and take it over. The deal was consummated in 1934 for a price of $175.

Gus grew up learning the business, at his father's side from the age of eight. He was nineteen in 1951 when he took over the cart. Three years later, Gus married Stella Bistolas on Valentine's Day. Kalarais admitted that the wedding date was kind of corny but also practical: obviously, the wedding would have had to take place in the off-season.

The *yiayia* in the cart's name, which means "grandmother" in Greek, originally referred to Pauline, Gus's mother. When Pauline died in 1992, Stella stepped into the role of the cart's *yiayia*. She became as well known as her husband; when she died in 2016, more than five hundred people attended her funeral.

Operating the cart takes a lot of work. Kalaris will work from dawn until after dark; it takes a few hours just to prepare the cart for business each morning. All of the dozen or so syrups are homemade. And shaving huge blocks of ice for ten to twelve hours a day, and with an ice scraper that is almost as old as Gus is, is rough duty.

Fortunately, Kalaris has had scores of young men willing to work with him in the summer. People like Michael Spanos, Bill Harold, Ryan Bickert and more—some work a few days a week, while others have worked regularly for several summers. They take money, make change, shovel popcorn into boxes and take orders for Kalaris to fill.

The one thing they don't do, however, is shave ice. That is Kalaris's job. It's exhausting work, but he doesn't seem to mind. There was a time when the cart would remain open until 11:00 p.m., but in recent years, Kalaris began to close up shop at 9:00 p.m., his lone concession to age.

He said that he continues to operate the cart also because he loves satisfying people, and he has a loyal following. People bringing their children and grandchildren to get an ice ball can remember their parents or grandparents bringing them to the cart.

And the fans aren't limited to people either. One of Gus's regulars is a dachshund that stops by every now and then for a lemon snow cone. "Every time he comes here he looks up at me," Kalaris said. "I put the ice in a cup, and he looks at me again, and then we go over there [pointing to a grassy area] and he gets his lemon cone. I don't know why he got hooked on the lemon," he added with a laugh.

Kalaris knows most of the regulars by face, fewer by name. "I know a lot of people's names, but I can't remember them all," he said. "Someone will come up to me and say, 'Do you remember so-and-so,' and I'll say, 'Oh, yeah!,' but half the time I don't anymore."

But whether he remembers them or not, his customers love him and look out for him. In 2018, when road construction closed the West Ohio Street Bridge, a social media blitz alerted people to the fact that Kalaris's business was hurting. It started with a three-minute video shot by videographer Willy James and posted on Facebook, and people responded. At about the same time, according to an article by journalist Neil Strebig, Mark Fatla, the executive director of the Northside Leadership Conference, worked with the city planners to create a "loop" so that vehicles could get to Kalaris's cart.

Kalaris is so well respected in the area that, as rough-and-tumble as the Northside can be, no one has ever attempted to rob him.

Kalaris grew up in the same neighborhood as the Rooney family, and Gus loves to point out to people the bench where Dan Rooney would sit and autograph people's popcorn boxes. Kalaris noted that the Rooneys "had the biggest business on the Northside, and I had the smallest."

But not so small that Kalaris can't give back to the community that has had his back all these years. After Stella Kalaris died in 2017, he set up the Gus and Yiayia's Scholarship, part of the Northside Leadership Conference Scholarship Fund, in her honor.

Kalaris has been featured in numerous newspaper and magazine articles, as well as a few news documentaries. He and his wife were honored by Pittsburgh City Council in 2012 when April 25 was declared Gus and Yiayia Day. But the biggest honor, as far as Gus is concerned, is the honor of having generations of families from around the city visit him in the spring and summer, year after year. After all, to his customers, Gus Kalaris is like their padou—Greek for grandfather.

Rick Sebak: Pittsburgh's Storyteller

Rick Sebak is not a historian. He's quick to correct anyone who refers to him this way. When he attended the University of North Carolina–Chapel Hill, he studied English and theater, finally settling on broadcast communications.

What Rick Sebak is, however, is a storyteller. In fact, he is Pittsburgh's preeminent spinner of tales, almost all of them about the city in which he was born and raised.

Sebak has been the driving force behind more than forty documentaries about Pittsburgh and Pennsylvania. Beginning with *The Mon, The Al & The O* in 1988, Sebak and his WQED crew have introduced Pittsburghers to everything from neighborhoods (*The Strip Show*, *North Side Story*, *Something About Oakland*) to bridges (*Flying Off the Bridge to Nowhere!*) to buildings (*Houses Around Here*). They've taught people about *Stuff That's Gone* to *Things That Are Still Here* to *Things We've Made*. They've examined hot dogs and sandwiches and other foods available in *Pennsylvania Diners and Other Roadside Restaurants*. He is becoming quite famous as the host of *Nebby: Rick Sebak's Tales of Greater Pittsburgh*, a series of thirty-minute shows available for streaming on WQED's website.

And it all came about because of a phone call a friend in Colorado made to Sebak in 1988 about a job opening in the Steel City. Otherwise, he might be celebrated today as South Carolina's best storyteller.

Sebak is a native Pittsburgher, having grown up in Bethel Park. But after graduating from Bethel Park High School in 1971, he left to attend college at UNC. "I was reading *Look Homeward, Angel* when I was applying to college," Sebak explained. "Thomas Wolfe went to Chapel Hill, and the way he described it…so I applied there. More than any other place I had applied, they were excited to have me. Accepted me into the honors program and blah, blah, blah."

Rick Sebak in his Mini Cooper, outside Emil's in Rankin, his favorite restaurant. *Photo by author.*

Sebak originally intended to study English and theater—he came from a theater background, his mother having helped found the local community theater in Bethel Park. But theater ironically led him to television. "As theater majors, we had to intern at a TV workshop in Raleigh," he said. "On Saturday mornings, we would go to Raleigh, and whatever they needed us to do, we would do. I thought the teacher was great, and I said I want to take classes with him. But to take his classes you had to be an RTVMP (radio, television and motion pictures) major."

So, Sebak changed his major and never looked back. His mother helped cement Rick's relationship with television when she sent him a clipping from the *Pittsburgh Press*.

"Barbara Holsopple did a column, kind of a gossip column," he said. "This piece said that Josie Carey was doing a children's soap opera in South Carolina." Before moving to the South, Carey—another Pittsburgh native— was well known to Pittsburghers for her show *The Children's Corner* and for her work with Fred Rogers at WQED.

Sebak wrote to Carey, asking if he could do a summer internship with her. Carey agreed, and Sebak's future in television was ensured. After the internship, Sebak studied in Europe for a year. When he returned, he went back to work with Carey until her program was canceled.

After he graduated, Sebak was contacted by South Carolina ETV— the umbrella for PBS stations in the state—with a job offer as an associate

Editor Rick Manoogian, *left*; producer Minette Seate; and Rick Sebak. *Rick Sebak.*

producer on an energy conservation project. That was the start of a relationship with public broadcasting that has lasted to this day.

One of Sebak's favorite pastimes is reading, which he parlayed into a gig writing book reviews for the *Columbia State*. This led to a bit of serendipity when he was asked to do reviews on TV on an early-morning news show. John Anderson, the host of another program, *Carolina Journal*, liked Sebak's style and approached him to do reviews on his program, "where you'll get a bigger audience." Rick ended up with a bigger audience, all right, but not as a book reviewer.

"I did two, and then John said to me, 'You ride your bike to work every day. I'd like to do a story about that. I'll give you a cameraman and an editor.'" And Sebak never did another book review, as his career spun off in a now-familiar direction.

"I started doing stories about little things I liked about Columbia, like doing the *New York Times* crossword puzzle in the coffee shop," he recalled. "Every summer I would walk up and down the beach with a cameraman, looking for people who were reading, and I asked them about what they were reading. It was always fun and interesting and unpredictable."

Sebak continued doing short pieces until a trip to see his father became the catalyst for creating and producing documentaries. "My dad got sick, and I decided to go to see him," Sebak said. "My cameraman [Buck Brinson] said, 'I'm going to ride with you.' On the trip, he said, 'We need to do a long documentary.' The state had just named a swing dance, called the shag, as the official state dance. So we decided to do a documentary on that."

The call to "come home," as it were, came in 1988. Rick and Buck had just returned from twenty-eight days in Australia, where they were covering the premiere of the Down Under version of the Spoleto Festival, a performing arts festival that was founded in 1977 in Charleston, South Carolina, by Italian composer Gian Carlo Menotti.

"A friend in Denver called me and told me about an ad in *Broadcasting* magazine for a TV producer in Pittsburgh," Sebak said. "It was at WQED. I went up to the city and interviewed with eight different people, and at the end of the day they offered me the job, which I was not prepared for. I told them I needed six weeks to make a decision."

Well, everyone in Pittsburgh knows what his answer was, and after thirty-five years Sebak can still say, "I have never regretted my decision. It's been a good ride. Pittsburgh is eternally surprising, which is my favorite thing about it."

Most people will admit that as much as they love their jobs, there is always one or two elements of it that they'd rather not have to do. Not Rick Sebak. He says he can't think of a single aspect of creating a documentary that he doesn't like—although he does acknowledge "a bit of post-partum depression" after the process has been completed.

"Documentaries are a segmented process," Sebak explained. "There's the research, the planning and the shooting, and then the editing. I love the blend of those different things, the joy of seeing it all come together. Librarians have been such a great help to me. They know so many secrets. You just have to keep asking questions. At the same time, I love setting things up and taking the crew on the shoot."

The easy-going Sebak admits that there are a few things regarding his profession that he doesn't like to do. One is investigative journalism. "People ask me, 'Don't you want to do a hard-hitting *60 Minutes*–style story?' and I say no. There are plenty of people doing that," he noted. "I love the niche that I work in. I'm generally talking with people about things they love."

The second is interviewing celebrities. "I haven't done a lot of stuff with celebrities because I think it's more fun to talk with people who aren't used to being interviewed." However, he has fond memories of interviewing Fred Rogers. Talking with his mentor, Josie Carey, about Mr. Rogers "was a gem of an interview." And he went on air with Wendy King, who insisted that the interview be conducted in the attic of her Greentree home, where she kept all of the *Party Line* memorabilia. "I had to go through the closet in her bedroom to get to the attic," he recalled. "That was magical."

The third is filming in sterile environments. Sebak wants to be where the people are. "We would never ask a restaurant or other business to shut down, like they do on *Diners, Drive-Ins & Dives*," he said. "We would never do that. We live for the comments from people."

The fourth is naming the favorite of all his documentaries. "I tell people I don't really have one. It's like, which of your children do you love the most." But Sebak will admit that he has "a greater affection" for the local things he's done over the fifteen or so national shows he has shot for PBS.

Working with PBS was a wonderful experience, but he said it was hard to crack the national scene. "*Pennsylvania Diners* was what got me national exposure," Sebak recalled. "I had always asked PBS if they would consider running one of my documentaries, and they would say, 'It's too local, too parochial. Only you people in Pittsburgh care about this stuff.' But *Pennsylvania Diners* got their attention. It was ninety minutes long. They said, 'Cut it down to sixty and we'll run it.'"

"The show got good ratings," he said. "They asked me, 'What else could you do? Make us a list of ten things you'd like to do.'" Sebak said he believes that PBS ended up doing all ten. "*A Hot Dog Program* and *Great Old Amusement Parks* were the first times I was given the ability to hand-pick my crew," Sebak remembered. "I realized just how important that was to me. It made the whole experience even more pleasant, traveling the country and meeting people and seeing all that we did."

"Looking back, we didn't realize just how cool it was that we got to do all these. It was a plum assignment, but we looked at it as work. Only now do we think, like, wow, we even went to Alaska!"

Although he is the "voice" of the documentaries, Sebak is seldom seen on camera—despite having a cherubic face and a smile that lights up a room. He is not particularly comfortable having the spotlight on him. He acknowledges the debt he owes to people like Minette Seate, his trusted sidekick and producer; Kevin Conrad, his editor for thirty-three years; Rich Capaldi, the man who has taken Conrad's place; director of photography Frank Caballero; and dozens more.

Bob Lubomski, *left*, and Buck Brinson assist Rick Sebak during one of his interviews. *Rick Sebak.*

"I get so much credit for what I do, but it is totally a collaborative effort," Sebak noted. "I rely so much on camera people and sound people, and I am always grateful to those people who do the work I get credit for. To not acknowledge them would be almost criminal."

Part III
SPORTS

Myron Cope: The "Terrible Towel" Man

Myron Cope was one of the greatest sportswriters of his or any era. But most Pittsburghers don't remember him for his articles in *Sports Illustrated*, for his award-winning profiles of Muhammed Ali or Howard Cosell or even his book, *The Game that Was: The Early Days of Pro Football*.

Nope. Yinzers—and members of Steelers Nation around the globe—hold Myron dear to their hearts for a gimmick: the Terrible Towel, a simple piece of terrycloth that would be often imitated but never surpassed in the annals of professional sports. The Towel would cement Cope's legacy in Pittsburgh, even more than his thirty-five years of broadcasting Steelers football.

But if it hadn't been for the folks at WTAE-AM radio giving him a chance to do sports commentaries, Myron Sidney Kopelman might have become just another Pittsburgh sportswriter. And the Terrible Towel might never have come to be.

Make no mistake, WTAE radio was going out on a limb in 1968 when it hired Cope. As erudite as he sounded on paper, even Cope would admit that his voice did not exactly have people begging him to do voiceovers. When Don Shafer, program director for WTAE, called him to discuss doing a five-minute sportscast every morning, Cope thought that someone was playing a joke on him.

But Shafer was not kidding. WTAE figured that Cope's knowledge of sports would override a voice that one news columnist likened to "a

Myron Cope, *center*, in the Steelers broadcast booth with Tunch Ilkin, *left*, and Bill Hilgrove. *Pittsburgh Steelers*.

tornado ripping through a junkyard." And he would be on the air for only a few minutes.

The radio executives almost miscalculated, however. For the first two weeks of Cope's tenure, people called the station demanding that Cope be taken off the air. But executives liked what they heard—the content, if not the voice—and they stuck with Cope. In time, people grew to tolerate Cope's sandpaper-y, nasal delivery because they came to love him.

Cope, it turned out, *was* Pittsburgh. Here was a local guy who called it like it was, in that unmistakable Western Pennsylvania dialect. He was an everyman, saying what many fans were thinking, and saying it in language they could relate to. Soon, "This is Myron Cope, on sports" became one of the most well-known pronouncements in Pittsburgh. His broadcasts, which morphed into nightly, hourlong talk shows, were the most listened-to sports shows for more than two decades.

"Myron had the greatest talk show in the world," said David Finoli, a sportswriter who has written or coauthored more than three dozen books on Pittsburgh's sports history. "There's nobody who even comes close. Myron made everything interesting, no matter what the subject. If I was listening while driving, I would stay in the car just to keep listening to him."

Cope slowly grew into his radio role, but that didn't mean he was comfortable there. So he was understandably perplexed two years later when the Pittsburgh Steelers came and asked him to be color commentator beside Jack Fleming on Steelers radio broadcasts. A five-minute broadcast, or even a radio show, was one thing, but having people listen to him for a four-hour-plus stretch (pre- and post-game shows, as well) was quite another. Besides, he once readily admitted to Steeler Hall of Famer Ernie Stautner, "I couldn't diagram a play on a blackboard if my life depended on it." And it was true; most color men then in the broadcast booth (and today virtually all) were former football players.

But Cope was a sportswriter. He might not have known as much about football as new head coach (and eventual neighbor) Chuck Noll did, but he knew the game well, he knew how to explain the action in a way the average fan understood and he knew when to second-guess a coach or player and when to keep quiet. And that would serve his purpose through thirty-five glorious years beside Jack Fleming (twenty-four years) and Bill Hillgrove (eleven years).

From day one, Cope was a fan, a fact that sometimes set him at odds with Fleming, one of the most low-key, professional announcers ever to call a ballgame. He would express his pleasure and disappointment with equal fervor, his voice rising and falling like a giant wave as he got worked up and then settled down. That was hard for Fleming to get used to, but the man tolerated it and eventually warmed to it, even though he himself would never broadcast his emotions over the air. Like many people who came in regular contact with Cope, Fleming and he became close friends.

"Myron brought you into the game," said Finoli, who met Cope when he was attending Duquesne University and he and Cope were covering Duquesne Dukes basketball. "He got you excited. It was a different way to see the game. I had fun, win or lose, because of Myron. I always turned down the sound (on the TV) and listened to Myron and Fleming, Myron and Hillgrove."

Cope was never as colorful in his phraseology as Rosey Rowswell, Bob Prince or Mike Lange, but he loved to create his own way of referring to things. Where we might say "Wow," Cope would say "Yoi!" If the action was really impressive, he'd say "double yoi!" "Okel-dokel" was his way of saying something was okay with him. He would address callers to his talk show with "How do?" If he thought something was BS, he'd call it "garganzola."

He also liked giving players and teams nicknames. For example, he referred to Steeler linebacker Jack Lambert as "Jack Splat." Kordell Stewart was "Slash," and Jerome Bettis was "The Bus." Cope loved calling rival teams disparaging names, like the Cincy Bungles, Cleve Brownies and Denver Yonkos.

Once, during a game against the Washington Redskins, Cope referred to the team as the "Wash Redfaces," which allegedly caused Redskins owner Dan Snyder to send one of his minions to the broadcast booth at halftime to tell Cope to knock it off. That was the wrong thing to do. After Cope and Hillgrove went back on the air, not only did Cope tell fans what had occurred, he continued, "If that boy billionaire thinks he can shut me up, he should stick his head in a can of paint!"

There is one phrase that Cope did not come up with, although he was responsible for promulgating it. On the evening of December 23, 1972, after Steelers rookie Franco Harris scooped a ball out of the air and ran it into the end zone to rally Pittsburgh to a playoff victory against the Oakland Raiders, a fan by the name of Michael Ord was celebrating the victory with friends. He reportedly raised his glass and said to his friends, "This night will forever be known as the Feast of the Immaculate Reception." Then he told a friend, Sharon Levosky, to "call Myron Cope."

She called Cope in the WTAE newsroom and related the story. Cope thought about it, and then, on the eleven o'clock news that evening, used the phrase on the air to describe the play. In his book, *Double Yoi!*, Cope wrote this: "Having conferred upon Franco's touchdown its name for 11 o'clock news viewers to embrace, I accept neither credit nor, should you hold the moniker to be impious, blame."

But the object with which Cope will forever be identified is the Terrible Towel. The Terrible Towel was introduced in December 1975, before a home playoff game against the Houston Oilers. To be fair, the Towel was not Cope's idea. It was suggested to him as a gimmick by a sales guy at WTAE, whose executives that felt they needed some sort of symbol to fire up football fans. But Cope quickly embraced the idea, came up with the name and introduced it on a newscast a week before the playoff game. He suggested that fans attending the game bring either a gold or black towel with them to wave.

When fans showed up at Three Rivers Stadium on December 27, 1975, for the first round of the NFL playoffs, an estimated 60 percent of them were carrying gold or black towels. The Steelers won, 28–10, on the way to their second Super Bowl, and the Terrible Towel followed them every step of the way. It would never die. Many sports teams, from baseball to football to hockey, have tried their own rallying objects. But none has had the staying power of or been embraced by so many people as the Towel. It has become a symbol for the city around the world. The Terrible Towel has been waved or displayed virtually anywhere Pittsburghers or Steeler fans have gone, even at the summit of Mount Everest.

Myron Cope was astute enough to have the name and the Towel trademarked. He held—but never benefited from—the trademarks until 1996, when he donated them to the Allegheny Valley School for Exceptional Children in Coraopolis. (The Copes' autistic son, Danny, has lived at the school since he was fifteen.) Since then, sales from the Terrible Towel and all the ancillary products, such as ties and even earrings, have generated several million dollars for the school.

Cope has received awards few other sports announcers have been accorded. Shortly after he retired, he received the Pete Rozelle Radio-Television Award for his contributions to the art of football broadcasting. That same year, he became the first professional football announcer inducted into the Radio Hall of Fame.

For his writing, in 1987 he was named a "noted literary achiever" by the Hearst Corporation. Other people who have made that list? Mark Twain, Jack London and Walter Winchell.

When Cope died, on February 27, 2008, tributes poured in from far and wide. Steelers chairman Art Rooney II said that "history will remember him

Cope being honored at halftime of a Steelers game. *Pittsburgh Steelers.*

as one of the great sportscasters of any era." Luke Ravenstahl, Pittsburgh's mayor at the time, recalled Cope as "the heartbeat of the Pittsburgh Steelers in many ways." On February 29, the day of his funeral, hundreds of fans stood at Pittsburgh City Hall to honor Cope. The funeral, however, was private, its location unannounced.

By way of explanation, Bob Smizik of the *Post-Gazette* wrote, "Had the secret of the service and its site not been kept, tens of thousands would have descended on the Slater funeral home in Greentree....Greentree and Cochran roads, the two main arteries leading to the funeral home, would have been parking lots."

DOCK ELLIS: THE LSD NO-HITTER

People say that it's unfair to judge a man by a single incident. And yet it would not be out of line to suggest that the night of June 12, 1970, perfectly summed up who Dock Ellis was: a brash, cocksure man who lived life his way, sometimes to excess and more often than not using bad judgment, but who had talent in abundance. June 12 was the evening Ellis pitched a no-hitter for the Pittsburgh Pirates against the Dan Diego Padres—while allegedly high on LSD and amphetamines.

Ellis was a right-handed pitcher who began and ended his career with the Pirates. His career win-loss record was 138-119, with a 3.46 ERA and 1,136 strikeouts. In addition to the Pirates, Ellis played for the New York Yankees, Oakland Athletics, Texas Rangers and New York Mets. He retired in 1979 and passed away in 2008 of liver disease brought on by substance abuse.

Ellis, born in Los Angeles in 1945, excelled at baseball and basketball. After graduating from Gardena High School, he attended a junior college and played semipro ball with the Pittsburgh Pirates Rookies. Its manager, Chet Brewer, was a scout for the Pirates, and he convinced the Pirates in 1963 to sign the kid to a contract. That was fine with Ellis; he reportedly snubbed several other ball clubs, holding out for an offer from Pittsburgh because he had heard that the Bucs offered a $60,000 signing bonus.

But the poor choices that would plague his life cost him money. Before Ellis could sign the contract, he was caught stealing a car. He was given probation, but the Bucs, now leery of this troubled youth, offered him $500 a month and only a $2,500 signing bonus.

Dock Ellis being mobbed after completing his no-hitter against the San Diego Padres.
Pittsburgh Pirates.

Ellis worked in the minors for the next four-plus seasons. In 1968, he started the season in Columbus with the Pirates' AAA farm club. In June, he was brought up by the Pirates to be a middle reliever. But by season's end, he had proven to be an effective starter, and he was part of the starting rotation in 1969. His numbers weren't great that year: 11-17, with a 3.56 ERA. But in 1970 he led the Pirates in wins with 13, even though he missed more than a month of the season due to arm soreness.

On June 12, 1970, the normally sunbaked city of San Diego was in the midst of its infamous "June Gloom." The day was cloudy and cool, with a misty rain falling on and off throughout the day, and it was breezy. At two o'clock in the afternoon, the Pirates, who had had Thursday off after flying from San Francisco to San Diego, were no doubt organizing themselves before making their way to San Diego Stadium for a twi-night doubleheader.

All, that is, except Ellis. Ellis was about 120 miles northwest of the city, in Los Angeles. He had been given permission the previous day to travel home, after being reminded that he was scheduled to pitch the first game of the evening.

But at 2:00 p.m. that day, Ellis was being roused from a drug- and alcohol-induced stupor at a friend's house in LA. At first, he had no idea it was Friday. He had been on an LSD trip since shortly after leaving San Diego Thursday. He pulled himself together, got to the airport and boarded a 3:00 p.m. flight south. He landed at about 4:30 p.m. and headed straight to the ballpark. He was still high on acid, only now he had compounded his situation by taking speed in the hopes of counteracting the LSD.

That evening, Ellis was a train wreck that somehow never happened. Years later—the fact that he was high on the mound didn't become public knowledge for another fourteen years—Ellis would tell of the strange goings-on during that game. He said the baseball appeared to him as large as a balloon one pitch and as small as a golf ball the next pitch. Sometimes it would look like a comet coming off his hand. He thought Richard Nixon was the plate umpire. He admitted that he could barely see the batters, and had catcher Jerry May not been wearing reflective tape on his fingers, Ellis would not have been able to make out the pitch signs.

He was wild that night, as you might imagine. He walked eight batters and hit another. He was bailed out a few times by great fielding plays, most notably in the seventh inning when second baseman Bill Mazeroski made a backhanded stab of a low line drive. But a no-no is a no-no, no matter the condition of the pitcher on the mound.

The no-hitter was hardly the only thing that would distinguish Ellis's career. In 1971, he went 19-9 with a 3.02 ERA and made the national League All-Star team. Cincinnati manager Sparky Anderson even selected him to start the game, opposite Oakland A's pitcher Vida Blue.

That October, he would be member of the World Series Champion Pirates, after Pittsburgh beat the Baltimore Orioles 4 games to 3. Ellis would pitch Game 1, losing to Dave McNally, and would become part of the answer to a baseball trivia question: How many different starting pitchers did the Pirates use in the 1971 World Series? (The answer: 6.)

He would pitch in Pittsburgh for four more years until he was traded to the Yankees after the 1975 season. Ellis always maintained that he enjoyed his time in Pittsburgh, so much so that when he decided to retire in 1979 he asked the New York Mets to trade him to the Pirates before the end of the season so that he could "die as a Pirate."

But his time in Pittsburgh was certainly not trouble-free. Controversy seemed to follow him, even when he wasn't trying to create it. For example,

Ellis often wore curlers in his hair to style it. Sometimes he would wear the curlers while in pre-game warm-ups, but never during a game. Still, when pictures began to circulate of Ellis in curlers in the bullpen, it earned him a talking-to from the Pirates on behalf of Major League Baseball: don't do that again. It was one of many times during his career that he would accuse MLB of racism. But it also earned him a photo spread of his hairstyles in *Ebony* magazine.

In 1972, while attempting to enter Riverfront Stadium before a game against the Cincinnati Reds, Ellis was pepper-sprayed by a security guard when he couldn't provide identification. According to Ellis, he tried to show the guard his World Series ring as ID. According to the guard, Ellis acted drunk, cursed at him and threatened him with his closed fist. Ellis was charged with disorderly conduct. He sued the Reds and the Reds sued him, but all was forgiven before the matter ever came to trial.

Of course, Ellis was pretty good at creating his own trouble. Facing the Reds in a 1974 game at Three Rivers Stadium, Ellis decided to hit every Reds batter, in retaliation for what he believed was the team's "intimidation" of the Pirates. Pete Rose stepped to the plate to start the game, and Ellis drilled him in the ribs. Joe Morgan was next; he took a pitch in the side. Dan Driessen followed—he got it in the back. Bases were loaded, but Ellis didn't care. Tony Perez was the next batter and Ellis walked him, but only because Perez was nimble enough to avoid four pitches. Strangely enough, it took two more pitches aimed at the head of Johnny Bench before Manager Danny Murtaugh came out and rescued the Reds from Ellis. Despite MLB's more lenient approach to head-hunting pitchers back then, it also was surprising to some that umpires did not intervene during Ellis's assault.

In spite of his talent, Ellis finally wore out his welcome with the Pirates in 1975. Late that season, Murtaugh decided that he wanted Ellis to pitch out of the bullpen. Ellis refused. Murtaugh asked him again the next night. Ellis refused once more, so the Pirates suspended him for one game. At a team meeting the next day, Ellis verbally attacked his manager, who ordered him out of the clubhouse. He was suspended for thirty days and fined $2,500, but Ellis came out of the doghouse on August 30 when he apologized to Murtaugh. But things were never the same again, and in December, he was traded to the Yankees.

After he retired early in 1980, Ellis finally went to rehab and got himself clean. In 1984, when he told his story about the LSD no-hitter, he said that he never pitched under the influence of that drug again. But he admitted that he never pitched sober; he always took amphetamines before he took the mound. Ellis said the one time he tried to pitch without the boost from uppers, in 1973, he became so unglued that he had to go back into the locker for his hit of speed.

Once he got clean, Ellis became a drug counselor. But the drugs and alcohol had done their damage. In 2007, he was diagnosed with cirrhosis of the liver. While waiting for a transplant, he developed heart failure, which negated his eligibility for a new liver. He died in 2008 at the age of sixty-three.

There are players and reporters who dispute Ellis's account of his no-hitter. People at that game, for example, stated that he didn't seem particularly out of sorts, and others questioned whether it would even be possible to accomplish such a feat while under the influence of LSD.

This writer believes Ellis's story. He would have no reason to make up the incident, and he was not known in any case for embellishment. Also, Ellis never bragged about the fact. Rather, he seemed embarrassed by the whole thing. In any case, we'll never know the truth, but it does make for a colorful tale.

MIKE LANGE: "ELVIS HAS LEFT THE BUILDING"

For someone who didn't see his first hockey game until he was twenty, Mike Lange has made quite a name for himself as a hockey play-by-play announcer. And for a man who grew up in California, Lange has made himself quite at home in Pittsburgh, and fans love him for it.

Such is his stature in the city and within the Pittsburgh Penguins organization that in 2020, when Lange decided to step down from the broadcast booth, the Penguins wouldn't just let him ride off into the sunset. They made him broadcaster emeritus. That's what you do for a man who has been associated with your team for an astounding forty-six years.

Mike Lange thrived in Pittsburgh because he is one of the most dynamic announcers in hockey. Lange knows the game like few other broadcasters and conveys that knowledge to fans in a crisp voice that has just a tinge of gravel to it.

And to think that when he was invited to his first hockey game, in 1969, he admitted to his friend, "I don't know a blue line from a red line." But he learned. Boy, did he learn.

Lange grew up in Sacramento, California, always knowing that he wanted to be a broadcaster one day. He attended Sacramento State University, where he earned a degree in broadcasting. While at Sac State, he was part of a student crew that did play-by-play of college baseball, football and basketball on campus station KERS-FM. His passion was baseball, but fate had other plans.

He remembers a friend, Glenn Shapiro, coming to his apartment one winter evening looking for someone to go with him to a local hockey game. Actually, as it turned out, what he wanted was someone to help him work at the game. "He came to the apartment around 5:30 p.m. and asked if anyone wanted to go to a hockey game," Lange recalled. "Everyone said they couldn't make it. He looked at me, and I told him, 'I don't know a blue line from a red line.' He looked me right in the eye and said, 'You never know.'"

So, Lange agreed to go, and he ended up being the penalty box timekeeper for the game, the teams for which were part of the Sacramento Ice Hockey Association. "They had about three hundred to four hundred people come to these games," Lange said. "And one of the things I noticed was the PA announcer, Danny, was doing play-by-play as well." This intrigued Lange, who was used to hearing PA announcers simply relaying basic information for fans, such as who scored and who committed a foul or made an error.

"I finished up that year, and the next year I went back and the league asked me if I would do the play-by-play," Lange explained, "because Danny wanted ten dollars a game, and we can only pay you five.' I said, 'Five dollars? That's fantastic!'" And just like that, Lange was a hockey announcer.

The previous season, the league had asked the Sac State broadcasting department if KERS would broadcast the league's playoff games. Lange's academic advisor declined the request. But the following year, with one of his students in the booth, the professor agreed, and Lange and Shapiro teamed up to do the playoffs.

After graduating, Lange went to Phoenix and landed a job working with veteran broadcaster Al McCoy, doing games for the Phoenix Roadrunners of the Western Hockey League. He worked with McCoy for three years before heading to San Diego as broadcaster for the Gulls, also of the WHL. (McCoy also left the Roadrunners, becoming the play-by-play man for the Phoenix Suns of the National Basketball Association. McCoy and Lange would eventually share something else in common—longevity in the booth. After fifty-one years, McCoy still does Suns broadcasts, the longest tenure of any broadcaster in the NBA.)

Lange's path to the Penguins was a little strange. In 1974, hearing that the team was looking for an announcer, he sent them a demo tape, and after several conversations with team executives, he was hired—without ever having set foot in Pittsburgh. "But it was a major step up and a great opportunity," Lange said. "So, I flew from San Diego to Pittsburgh on Allegheny Airlines, an all-nighter. And I got off onto the tarmac in Pittsburgh because they didn't have gates back then, and then it hit me. I said, 'What is that smell?'" Lange had gotten an industrial introduction to the Steel City.

Lange soon learned something about the people of Pittsburgh that helped endear the city to him. "I couldn't believe how nice people are," he said. "They are so willing to help. And when you come to Pittsburgh, you need help. Just trying to drive around this city. People are helpful like they've been in the same situation before, and that's part of the beauty of it. And they are loyal. They love you to death, and it's mutual for me."

But Lange quickly discovered that Pittsburghers had not yet fallen in love with the Penguins. The Pirates were just three years removed from their last World Series victory, and the Steelers would be headed to their first Super Bowl before the year was out. The Penguins? The team would manage to make the playoffs that season before ignominiously blowing a 3-0 series lead against the New York Islanders. But the franchise was struggling financially, and the IRS would padlock the team's offices after the playoffs—and Lange would lose his job.

Fortunately for Penguin fans, Lange missed the city and the team. One year later, with the franchise on more solid footing financially, Lange applied for, and got, his old job back.

In his "rookie" season, Lange found himself up against two of the best broadcasters in professional sports. KDKA had the Gunner, Bob Prince, calling Pirates games, while WTAE had as its color man for Steelers games the inimitable Myron Cope. Lange learned of these men's penchants for colorful phrases, and he also knew of the reputation of the man Prince replaced, Rosey Rowswell. He was going to need some serious word ammunition if he were going to win over the fans.

So, he reached out to his mentor, McCoy, whose signature phrase was "Great balls of fire!" Knowing that McCoy had "retired" the phrase when he moved over to Suns broadcasts, Lange asked him if he could use it. McCoy gave Lange his blessing, and he used that as the first of what is now a veritable dictionary of sayings.

Over time, he would collect phrases. "I came up with some. People would call me and suggest some. I'd keep them all in a big shoe box, and at the end of the year I'd go through them and see which ones worked and which ones didn't."

In any given year, Lange says, he has about forty different phrases he can call on. Some hang on, year after year, and there isn't a true Penguins fan who can't rattle off at least five or six of them. From "Hallelujah Hollywood" to "Elvis has left the building!," Lange-isms have permeated Pittsburgh's culture.

If Lange can be said to have a signature, it could be his style of announcing a Penguins goal: "Heeeeeeee shoots and scores!" delivered in his iconic gravelly tone. But, as Lange claims, "They are all favorites. It's a long year when you're doing any major sport. You gotta break it up a little bit. That was my outlet." He adds that he is very careful about choosing which phrase to use and when.

Some of them make sense in context. For example, he might announce that the puck is about to be dropped to start the game by saying, "Get in the fast lane, Grandma. The bingo game is ready to roll." He'll let you know that a player is really happy about a play he made with the phrase, "He's smiling like a butcher's dog." Did a Penguin just embarrass an opposing goalie with a wild shot? "He smoked him like a bad cigar!"

Some phrases are fairly common: "He doesn't know whether to cry or wind his watch!" "Just one look, that's all it took!" Some are specific to a player, such as "Slap me silly, Sidney!" and "Make me a milkshake, Malkin!" And others just make no sense at all. "Scratch my back with a hacksaw!" "Shave my face with a rusty razor!" "Let's go hunt moose on a Harley!"

Phraseology aside, Lange is one of the most skilled hockey announcers around. But it wasn't easy for a man whose preferred broadcasting choice would have been baseball. "It takes about five years to really become comfortable and knowledgeable," he explained. "I thought I had learned a lot about the game when I got to Phoenix. But I got in the booth and found out I didn't. Because on a pro level it's a different animal, and there is so much to learn."

Lange did have an opportunity to do some baseball play-by-play in Pittsburgh. For the 1986 and 1987 seasons, he did play-by-play of Pirates games on cable TV with former Pirate pitcher Steve Blass doing color commentary.

In a 2021 interview with Jason Mackey of the *Post-Gazette*, Blass told him, "We would have made a hell of a team, I'll tell you that. I enjoyed every minute of it."

For his part, Lange has nothing but respect for Pittsburgh sportscasters. He said Bob Prince, who briefly called hockey games with Lange, "had a

Mike Lange being recognized for his years of service as Penguins hockey announcer. *Pittsburgh Penguins.*

tremendous influence on me. I worked with him for only a short time, but we struck up a nice friendship and I learned so much from him."

Lange retired in August 2021. Two months later, the Penguins held Mike Lange Night at PPG Paints arena. Among the tributes paid to the veteran was the naming of the arena's media level the Mike Lange Media Level. When he took the microphone during the pre-game ceremony, he told the fans, "I wish I could go another forty-five."

Pittsburgh undoubtedly feels the same.

BOB PRINCE: "WE HAD 'EM ALL THE WAY!"

Announcers can make or break the telecast of a baseball game, and this is even more so on a radio broadcast. Those broadcasters with the true gift of gab can make listeners almost feel like they are at the ballpark. They can manage to keep fans tuned in even when the game is slow or the home team is getting blown out.

In Pittsburgh, one of the best, and certainly the most colorful, announcers for Pirate games was the Gunner, Bob Prince. Love him or hate him, people listened to him. He was on the air for twenty-eight years, first as the partner of Rosey Rowswell and then as the play-by-play man alongside Jim "Possum" Woods and, later, Nellie King. When he died, in 1985, he left behind a cache of phrases and nicknames that likely will never be topped in Pittsburgh sports lore.

It was pure happenstance that Prince ended up in Pittsburgh. The son of Frederick Prince, a career army officer who had attended the U.S. Military Academy at West Point and played football for the Black Knights, young Bob attended more than a dozen schools around the country. The last, from which he graduated, was Schenley High School, in 1935. He then attended the University of Pittsburgh for a time, where he lettered in swimming, before enrolling in Stanford University in 1937. But he ultimately graduated from the University of Oklahoma with a degree in business administration. He then attended Harvard Law School but did not do well. So he returned to Pittsburgh, where he landed a job as the host of *Case of Sports* on WJAS radio. And just like that, his nomadic existence came to a close.

Prince would air his radio show each weeknight, while selling insurance as his "day" job. He was known for not being afraid to speak his mind, sometimes operating without a filter. It would create controversy on more than one occasion. He once ran afoul of local fighter Billy Conn when he accused Conn of avoiding top boxing opponents. Conn confronted Prince a few nights later, and according to a profile of Prince in the book *Sweet '60: The 1960 Pittsburgh Pirates*, Conn "decided he would settle the disagreement by slamming Prince against a wall and threatening to beat him senseless."

But incidents such as this were fine with Prince, who believed that any publicity is good publicity. He also adhered to the tenet that nothing was more important than making contacts and connections. That belief would benefit him in 1948, when a spot on the Pirates' broadcast team became available. Prince had the inside track on the job in part because he had made friends with Tom Johnson, one of the team's owners, when the two were at Harvard.

But Prince and Rowswell did not mesh well at the start. Prince loved his drink, and Rowswell

Bob Prince. *Wikimedia Commons.*

was a teetotaler. Prince was brash and loud, where Rowswell was not. In addition, Rowswell thought that Prince was out for his job, so it took a while for him to trust his partner. But once the initial skepticism wore off, the two worked well together for seven years until Rowswell's death in February 1955. Prince said that he learned much from his partner.

One of those things Rowswell taught Prince was to find offbeat, descriptive ways to describe a play. For example, Rowswell would announce a home run by yelling, "Open the window, Aunt Minnie! Here it comes!" A curveball that caused a batter to strike out was called "the old dipsy doodle." Prince took the cue from Roswell and eventually surpassed his partner and mentor in the colorful phrase department.

Prince's response to a home run was "You can kiss it goodbye!" When the Pirates won, whether the game was a blowout or a come-from-behind thriller, Prince would intone, "We had 'em all the way!" If the Bucs needed a couple of runs to tie the game, Prince would tell fans, "We need a bloop and a blast."

When the Pirates played at Forbes Field, Prince even gave a name to the notoriously hard infield: "alabaster plaster." The stadium itself he called the "House of Thrills." The tiny size of insects played into his descriptions for close plays in "by a gnat's eyelash" and "close as fuzz on a tick's ear." And after the team moved to Three Rivers Stadium, with its artificial turf, when a ball reached the outfield and looked like it might result in extra bases for the batter, Prince would call the hit a "bug on the rug."

Household objects occasionally got into the mix. A double play, in Prince parlance, was a "Hoover." But if a batter swung at a pitch that was way out of the strike zone, the Gunner would inform you that "he couldn't hit that with a bed slat."

"Bob Prince is the guy you quote now," said David Finoli, author of *The Pittsburgh Pirates: Images of Baseball*. "He had all the sayings. And he was the ultimate homer. I don't like when a guy gets in there and tries to be neutral. I want you to root for my team. When Bob Prince got excited, you knew there was a reason to be excited."

Prince became a friend to a lot of the players, something that does not always happen for announcers. Because he spoke Spanish, he was very helpful getting Latin American players acclimated to life in baseball and in the United States. He was particularly close with Roberto Clemente, whom Prince called the "Great One"—so much so that only Prince could get away with calling Clemente "Bob" or "Bobby."

He gave several players besides Clemente nicknames during his tenure. Prince called pitcher Vernon Law "The Deacon." (Law actually was an ordained minister in the Church of Jesus Christ of Latter-day Saints.) Gene Michael was "The Stick." Bob Bailey was "Beetle." Donn Clendenon was "Clink." There was Ed "Spanky" Kirkpatrick, Manny "Road Runner" Sanguillen and Dave "The Cobra" Parker.

He even gave a nickname to at least one opposing player. When Rusty Staub played for the Montreal Expos, Prince would call him "Le Grand Orange," a reference to Staub's thick shock of red hair and the Expos' location in French-speaking Quebec.

If Prince could be said to have a flaw, it was his penchant for telling long, sometimes rambling, stories. Some fans felt that he loved the sound of his voice more than he liked filling people in on the action on the field. But there was method to his madness, and he gave the credit again to his old partner Rowswell.

In *Sweet '60s*, Prince was quoted as saying, "Rosey taught me an important lesson. If you're losing 14–2 in the second inning, you've got to keep people interested with funny stories, names and reminiscences. You can't be worried about who hit .280 in 1943."

Prince also tried a few gimmicks during his time in the booth. Before the Steelers had the Terrible Towel, the Pirates had the Green Weenie and Babushka Power, courtesy of Prince.

The Green Weenie was born in 1966, in the aftermath of a game against the Houston Astros. During the game, Pirates trainer Danny Whelan was seen by Prince waving a green rubber hot dog at Astros pitcher Dave Giusti (who would later join the Pirates as a relief pitcher), yelling that Giusti was going to walk the next batter. Giusti did, and the Pirates ended up winning the game. Prince asked Whelan about it later and decided that he could promote Whelan's little toy as a good luck charm.

The official Green Weenie was a rattle that fans could buy and bring to the games. Directed at the Pirates, it was meant to be a good luck charm. Shake it at the opposition, though, and it became a hex sign. Prince was usually in control of when the Green Weenie would be brought out.

But apparently it was a little too gimmicky for Pittsburghers. Although the Green Weenie was around for part of the 1967 season, it eventually lost its appeal. The same was true of Babushka Power, black and gold hankies Prince introduced in 1974 in a similar vein. But you couldn't blame the guy for trying. Prince's job, as he saw it, was to get fans excited about the team and to get fans at home listening to the game.

However, not everyone was enamored of Prince's shtick, particularly his storytelling, and in the 1970s, Pirates general manager Joe L. Brown and

KDKA brass began monitoring the broadcasts more closely. They wanted Prince to remain more focused on the game and to do more to promote the ball club, although it was hard to say how much more the Gunner could have done.

But after more than two decades in the booth, Bob Prince was on thinner ice than he realized. On October 30, 1975, Westinghouse Broadcasting announced that it was firing Prince and Nellie King. Fans, and some advertisers, were shocked. Everybody, it seemed, wanted the duo back—except the executives at Westinghouse Broadcasting. A hastily arranged parade for Prince and King drew more than ten thousand fans. Local politicians and even current Pirate players spoke at a rally after the parade ended. But all it did was make the two men feel better about their place in fans' hearts.

Prince had some chances at broadcasting baseball after KDKA cut him loose. He worked with Gene Elston for a time, broadcasting Houston Astros games, and he was part of the three-man crew for the first season of *Monday Night Baseball*. But he wasn't happy in Houston, and he wasn't a good fit as the third wheel with Warner Wolf and Bob Uecker on MNB. He also tried his hand at broadcasting Penguins hockey games, but he couldn't keep up with the fast pace of the games.

Prince was diagnosed with cancer of the mouth in 1985. He had surgery to remove a tumor in April, but it would not stave off the cancer. He would die just two months later.

However, he would get one last chance in the Pirates broadcast booth, thanks to Lanny Frattare, one of the men who replaced him and King. He helped convince the Pirates and KDKA to bring Prince back. They gave him a three-year contract, causing Prince to remark, "They must have some faith in the Lord and me."

His return officially began in the fourth inning of a game against the LA Dodgers on May 3, 1985. Fans responded by waving Green Weenies and babushkas, and the Pirates scored nine runs that inning. They would win the game 16–2, a rare treat for fans who suffered that year through a 104-loss season.

But Prince's broadcasting stint would end on May 20, when he became ill and was rushed to the hospital. Doctors opted to stop his radiation treatments, and the Gunner died on June 10.

Milo Hamilton, the play-by-play man who replaced Prince, lasted just four years, having never been accepted by Pirates fans. But Frattare, who idolized Prince and who received much mentoring from the Gunner, would eventually surpass Prince's longevity. He spent thirty-three years as a Pirates broadcaster, retiring in 2009. He even created his own version of Prince's "We had 'em all the way!" call. After announcing the final score, Frattare would say, "And there was no doubt about it!"

Prince is honored in the Scribes and Mikemen wing of the Baseball Hall of Fame and received the Ford C. Frick Award for outstanding broadcasting in 1986.

Interestingly, although their careers overlapped by only a few years, there is a surprising connection between Prince and the late Steelers color analyst Myron Cope. Cope's son, Danny, lives at the Allegheny Valley School for Exceptional Children, and 100 percent of the proceeds from the sale of Terrible Towel Cope invented and its assorted merchandise benefit the school. Prince cofounded the school in 1960 and himself raised more than $4 million for the school in his lifetime.

Ringside Rosie: The Persona of Anna Buckalew

Every sport has its special brand of fan—loud, brash, dedicated and, sometimes, obnoxious. Duke University basketball has its Cameron Crazies. The Cleveland Browns have the Dawg Pound. And, for a time back in the '60s and '70s, professional wrestling in Pittsburgh had Ringside Rosie.

Ringside Rosie was the alter ego of Anna Buckalew, a wife and mother from the Northside. She lived not too far from the WIIC-TV studios (now WPXI) in Fineview, where, from 1958 to 1972, *Studio Wrestling* aired live every Saturday evening. Anna, whose nickname was given to her by the program's announcer, Bill Cardille, was front and center, more or less, every Saturday. She also appeared frequently at wrestling shows at the Civic Arena until her death in 1974.

A woman who said she had never been interested in wrestling until she heard about free tickets being given away at the studio, the bespectacled Buckalew plunked herself down in the front row and quickly grew to love the sport. She reportedly missed only two *Studio Wrestling* shows, both for family funerals, in sixteen years. Most weekends, she was accompanied by her friend and neighbor from across the way on Lestche Street, Margaret McFetridge.

Her antics amused fans, riled the wrestlers and possibly contributed as much to pro wrestling's popularity in Pittsburgh as the city's golden boy,

Bruno Sammartino. "She was just a big fan," Sammartino told *Pittsburgh Post-Gazette* sportswriter Mark Madden. "She was never part of the show, but I don't know how she got that front seat all the time, either."

"There was never anyone more enthusiastic than her," added John "Jumpin' Johnny" DeFazio.

Like any fan, Rosie had her favorite wrestlers, and there were those she loathed, and with Rosie you always knew which was which. She would shout encouragement to wrestlers like Sammartino or DeFazio, but for the "evil" ones, such as Killer Kowalski or George "The Animal" Steele, she would get physical: hit them with her purse, poke them with her umbrella or—God forbid!—stick them with a hat pin.

Now, if you think that no one would be so brazen as to commit assault with a stickpin, you would be wrong. Rosie was, and she likely got away with it because she was a woman, no matter how egregious the offense.

In his interview with Mark Madden in 1990, Sammartino told of a time when noted bad guy Baron Scicluna made a threatening move toward Rosie, as if to scare her. Bad idea, Baron. Rosie responded with a hat pin to his buttocks.

"I mean, Scicluna was really bleeding, but it was live TV, he had to go on," Sammartino was quoted as saying. "But he was obviously in pain during the match, and you could see the blood on his tights."

Like any good fan, Rosie saved some of her heckling for the fight officials. She directed some of her best stuff at Izzy Moidel, a referee who seems to have had his own shtick going on. Sometimes he would be overzealous in his officiating; other times it was almost as if he was blind. But whatever his attitude during a match, he—and we—knew that Rosie and her cohorts would let him have it.

"C'mon, Izzy! Let 'em wrestle!" "Hey Izzy! You're missing a good match. Open your eyes, ref!"

As you can imagine, Rosie had her share of critics. Some wrestlers disliked her because they thought she was getting more attention than they were. Others, obviously, had personal reasons. And there were those who believed that Anna Buckalew was paid to be Ringside Rosie. The producers of *Studio Wrestling* vehemently denied that Buckalew was on the payroll, and there was never any evidence to suggest otherwise.

Anna Buckalew died on May 25, 1974, at the age of seventy-two. Coincidentally, *Studio Wrestling* "died" a month later. Declining ratings and a desire by WIIC station owners to have the NBC affiliate taken more seriously as a news station had led to *Studio Wrestling*'s cancelation in 1972.

The program moved over to WPGH-TV, where it would muddle along for another two years before giving up the ghost.

For sixteen years, *Studio Wrestling* gave viewers a host of colorful characters, men with names that fit a certain persona and antics to match. But Ringside Rosie, aka Anna Buckalew, was the most authentically colorful of them all.

Tiger Paul and Mossie Murphy: The Cheerleaders

Paul Auslander and Maurice Murphy were distinctly different people. Murphy was a college graduate; Auslander was not. Murphy was a political consultant, while Auslander ran a newsstand and delivered newspapers before he moved to Las Vegas to work for a sports book.

But the two men had one thing in common. They were rabid fans, and unofficial cheerleaders, of their favorite college teams. At the University of Pittsburgh and Duquesne University, respectively, they were known as "Tiger Paul" and "Mossie Murphy."

Of the two, Tiger Paul was definitely the more colorful. He usually was dressed in a white shirt and tie, sometimes covered with a Pitt "letter sweater" and other times by a suit jacket and vest. He would run up and down the basketball court windmilling his arms, jump up and down or run in place and even belly flop on the court, all the while exhorting fans to get behind the Panthers.

Mossie was, relatively speaking, more reserved. He didn't leave his seat. He didn't show up in outlandish clothes. He had only one cheer. But when he stood up, the student body rose with him, and they shook the rafters of the old Civic Arena— and, later, Palumbo Center. But each was as well known as the players for which they cheered, and both died at a relatively young age.

Auslander was a short (five-foot-four) and pudgy native of Highland Park. He attended Peabody High School, and John Mehno, author of *The Best Pittsburgh Sports Arguments*, once described him as someone whose "zeal

"Tiger Paul" Auslander. *Wikimedia Commons.*

for playing sports exceeded his ability." He tried out for the high school football team and reportedly earned his nickname from a coach, who, in trying to make him try harder, yelled, "Be a tiger, Paul!"

But his inability to play well never diminished his zeal for athletics. He followed sports so much he set up a sports score service, providing information to bettors and bookies. He also coached summer league basketball, where he caught the attention of Tim Grgurich, at the time an assistant coach for the Panthers basketball team.

According to Auslander's obituary in the *Post-Gazette*, Grgurich saw that the young man had an innate ability to stir up fans. So he invited him to become an unofficial cheerleader for the Panthers.

Auslander's style was not for everyone. In fact, school administrators and Pitt's student cheerleading squad despised him. Administrators thought that he was a jerk, and the cheerleaders felt he upstaged them. At one game, things got so heated on the court that Pitt's cheerleading coach attacked Tiger Paul, ripping his shirt. The upshot? Auslander received an apology and a new shirt, and the coach eventually quit.

But the fans loved him, and once he became established it was nearly impossible to dislodge him. He would cheer for the team until 1982, and he influenced fans as well as bettors. It was said that the betting line on a Pitt basketball game would shift depending on whether Tiger Paul was on the sidelines for the game.

On occasion, Auslander's love of the Panthers would cause him to step over the line. During a game between Pitt and the West Virginia University Mountaineers, there was a bench-clearing brawl. Tiger Paul and the Mountaineer mascot joined the fray, getting into a wrestling match. At a game versus Temple University in Philadelphia, Tiger Paul was ejected when he got into an argument with a referee. But his scuffles just seemed to make fans love him even more.

Tiger Paul's cheerleading wasn't limited to the University of Pittsburgh. Auslander cheered with equal fervor at Pittsburgh Pirates baseball games at Three Rivers Stadium. He would mount the dugout roof and go into his routines, and the crowd would go wild. His antics attracted the attention of Atlanta Braves owner Ted Turner, who in 1976 tried to hire Auslander to move to Atlanta and do his shtick for the Braves.

Auslander turned him down, but Turner's overtures caused him to approach the Pirates about putting him on their payroll and bringing him on the road with the team. The Pirates demurred but offered to pay him fifteen dollars per game to continue rousing the fans at home. Auslander declined, rightly figuring that he could make more money as a stadium vendor, and his days as a Pirates cheerleader came to an end.

Tiger Paul's reign at Pitt ended six years later. On January 14, 1982, university officials asked him not to cheer at the basketball game that night against Duquesne. He agreed and did not cheer again for Pitt until the Eastern Eight basketball tournament two months later. After that, Auslander moved to Las Vegas and worked for several sports books over the years, reportedly with as much fervor as he did while cheering for the Panthers and the Pirates.

In late 1991, Auslander moved from Vegas to Reno to try to get a job there. He was last seen alive on February 22, 1992, and was discovered dead—apparently by his own hand—several days later in a room at the Carriage Inn. He was only forty-eight.

Mossie Murphy's tenure as a Dukes cheerleader was more distinguished, although his relationship with the university generated some controversy in the late 1980s. A native of Lawrenceville, Murphy graduated from Duquesne in 1957. While he was at Duquesne, two things became evident. One was his love of politics (he helped organized chapters of Students for Adlai Stevenson in 1955). The other was his passion for the Dukes basketball team. He used to lead the student section in a cheer he had created. It began with Mossie raising his arms as he chanted "Wohhhhhhh, Wohhhhhhh," which the students would echo. Then, shaking first one arm and then the other, as if he were holding pom-poms, he would continue with, "Shoo-shoo, rah-rah, shoo-shoo-rah-rah," as his fellow students mimicked him. This would be followed by another round of "wohhhh, wohhhhh." Mossie would finish by shouting, "Dukes!" and the crowd would respond with, "Let's go, Duquesne!" over and over, clapping five times after each chant.

After Murphy graduated, he continued to go to the games and do his now-famous cheer. Only now he sat across from the students. When he stood, his portly visage marked by his blue and red striped shirt and his mass of dark hair trailing down the back of his neck, the students—and many other fans—stood along with him, ready to follow his lead.

But Murphy's love for the Dukes went beyond his willingness to lead cheers during basketball season. In Murphy's obituary in 1997, university president John Murray was quoted as saying, "He was an unsolicited spokesman on behalf of the university for a long as anyone can remember."

Murphy would talk up the university every chance he got, and that included being an unofficial recruiter for the basketball team. His intentions were well meaning, but not always appreciated. In a 1967 *Sports Illustrated* column about Myron Cope, written by *SI* publisher Garry Valk, Murphy made it into the mix. Valk, in talking about Cope, wrote, "In January 1963 he unearthed a loud, corpulent basketball recruiter named Mossie Murphy who, in his devotion to Duquesne University kept thrusting star talent on the school while Duquesne Coach Red Manning kept shouting, 'Get that fat boy out of my hair!'"

In 1988, however, Murphy ran afoul of the NCAA by hiring a Duquesne sophomore, Pete Freeman of Rochester, Pennsylvania, for a job the previous summer. Murphy said that he hired Freeman as part of a project to learn the political views of eighteen- to twenty-five-year-olds. Freeman was paid $1,200 for about ninety hours of work.

In a case of he said/he said, Murphy told an NCAA investigator that he hired Freeman at the request of basketball coach Jim Satalin and that he did nothing "legally, ethically or morally wrong." Satalin said that he never discussed Freeman with Murphy and didn't even know that Freeman worked for the consultant until "two or three days" before the NCAA came calling.

The NCAA ruled that Freeman's job was a violation of NCAA regulations. It suspended Freeman for seven games and ordered him to pay a $1,200 fine to the charity of his choice. Freeman never played another game for the Dukes, transferring to the University of Akron the following year.

Mossie Murphy died on January 25, 1997, of a heart attack while playing golf in Hilton Head, South Carolina. He was only sixty-one. Interestingly, Murphy apparently long had the sense that he was destined to die young. In 1990, in a Q&A feature in the *Post-Gazette* called "Dossier," Murphy's answer to the question "Accomplishment you're proudest of" was "Living this long."

BIBLIOGRAPHY

Burstin, Barbara S. *Sophie: The Incomparable Mayor Masloff.* Pittsburgh, PA: Barbara Burstin Books, 2021.

Cope, Myron. *Double Yoi: A Half Century of Sportswriting and Broadcasting.* New York: Sports Publishing, 2013.

Gazarik, Richard. *Wicked Pittsburgh.* Charleston, SC: The History Press, 2018.

Goodman, Andrew. *Eighty Days: Nellie Bly and Elizabeth Bisland's History-Making Race Around the World.* New York: Ballantine Books, 2014.

Hall, Donald. *Dock Ellis in the Country of Baseball.* New York: Simon & Schuster, 1989.

Heineman, Kenneth. *A Catholic New Deal: Religion and Reform in Depression Pittsburgh.* University Park: Pennsylvania State University Press, 1999.

Kroeger, Brooke. *Nellie Bly: Daredevil, Reporter, Feminist.* New York: Three Rivers Press, 1995.

Parker, Clifton Blue, and Bill Nowlin. *Sweet '60: The 1960 Pittsburgh Pirates.* Phoenix, AZ: SABR, 2013.

Rimmel, William H. *The Allegheny Story.* Pittsburgh, PA: Guttendorf Press, 1981.

Wecht, Cyril H., and Jeff Sewald. *The Life and Deaths of Cyril Wecht: Memoirs of America's Most Controversial Forensic Pathologist.* Jefferson, NC: Exposit Books, 2020.

ABOUT THE AUTHOR

Paul King is the author of *Iconic Pittsburgh: The City's 30 Most Memorable People, Places and Things*. Paul is a native of Pittsburgh, raised on Mount Washington with a grand view of the three rivers, Point State Park, the Northside and the downtown skyline. A graduate of Duquesne University, he has been a journalist for more than forty years. He currently lives in Williston, Vermont, with his wife, Karen, but Pittsburgh will always be "home."